Hemmendinger, Judith.
  Survivors : children of the Holocaust / by Judith
Hemmendinger ; foreword by Elie Wiesel. -- Zenith ed.
-- Bethesda, Md. : National Press, c1986.
  149 p., [8] p. of plates : ill. ; 23 cm.

Translated from the French.
Includes bibliographical references.
03096874 LC:86012460 ISBN:0915765241 :

1. Holocaust survivors - France - Taverny - Biography.
2. Jewish children - France - Taverny - Biography. 3.
(SEE NEXT CARD)

SURVIVORS
Children of the Holocaust

by Judith Hemmendinger

Foreword by Elie Wiesel

A Zenith Edition
National Press, Inc.
7508 Wisconsin Ave.
Bethesda, Md 20814
(301) 657-1616

Library of Congress Cataloging-in-Publication Data

Hemmendinger, Judith.
    Survivors : children of the Holocaust.

    Translation of: Les enfants de Buchenwald.
    1. Holocaust survivors--France--Taverny--Biography.
2. Jewish children--France--Taverny--Biography.
3. Buchenwald (Germany : Concentration camp)
4. Taverny (France)--Biography.   I. Title.
DS135.F85T38413   1986   940.53'15'03924044367 86-12460
ISBN 0-915765-24-1

CONTENTS

5

FOREWORD

Dear Judith,

I read your book and I remember; I return to 1945 . . .
Ecouis, Ambloy, Taverny . . . the dumbfounded instructors
. . . the disoriented children. Did you know that to us, you
belonged to another universe? Everything separated us—
the language, the physical surroundings, and above all, the
memories.

Did you know, Judith, that we pitied you? You made us
pity you. You thought you could educate us, and yet the
youngest among us knew more than you of the value of
things, of the futility of life, and of the brutal triumph of
death. Impressed neither by your age nor your authority,
we watched you with amusement and mistrust. We felt that
we were stronger than you.

How did you do it, Judith, how did you tame us? Niny,
that young, beautiful and devoted teacher of whom you
speak so highly—how did she put up with us for so many
weeks? I regret our behavior; I am embarrased about it
now. We were hard on you; we made it hard for you to find
a path, a possibility of understanding yourselves and us.

I often dream of the months and years we lived at the
Children's Homes of the O.S.E. (a French children's welfare organization). The first Shabbat meals . . . the walks,
the campfires, the songs, the talks. . . . I will never forget the
grand festivals at Ambloy . . . reciting Kaddish together . . .
the fast on Yom Kippour. The joy—at first forced, then
genuine—of Simchat-Torah. I am sure that you recall all of
it well, Judith . . . the beginnings, the tears, the letters, the

7

dreams, the nightmares. We were all haunted by the same desire to win the wager: Moishe-Ber, Menashe, Kalman, Binem, Glick. One day, I, too, will try to relate, in my own way, all those stories which link us to yours.

And do you remember Chouchani? The Talmud lessons ... the stormy debates. Was it necessary to initiate us into modern life? Did we have to leave Earth a saint or rejoin a cousin in Brooklyn? I remember my first class report: The Ghetto—Danger or Temptation? I pronounced it in Yiddish. Andre Bodner advised me: "The design, do not forget the design." The choral group, I also remember the choral group. Intimidated by the children I directed, I had to feign violence in order to maintain my status. Each recital cost me nights of insomnia. I lacked self-assurance and authority; I could not turn away any boy or girl who wanted to sing with us, even if he or she sang badly. Moreover, I could not address myself to a girl chorister without lowering my eyes; all the girls were attractive and inaccessible. I must have appeared stupid; I realized it, but. . . .

Now I understand that you, the instructors, also had obstacles to surmount, problems to solve. Educating a group like ours, with such peculiarities and obsessions, was not easy; lacking guidelines probably made it even harder.

What it comes down to is that it was a challenge for both you and us. Logically, it was doomed to failure. How could we possibly work together, and for whose sake? Emerging from darkness, we had hardly succeeded in getting rid of it; moreover, we did not want to. Uprooted, underprivileged, we had faith only in death. This time, the survivors had nothing to say to the living. Europe and the rest of the world celebrated the victory over Hitler's Germany without us. Immured in the solitude of a destroyed childhood— robbed, humiliated—we wished to remain aloof. Each time a representative of the outside world tried to approach us, we withdrew further. We totally refused you. We did not want your help, your understanding, your psychological tests, your charity. You entered our lives too soon; we were still in mourning.

Really, Judith, we were condemned to live cloistered lives,

like those against the wall. Yet, in a short time, we succeeded in rediscovering our direction. How does one explain this miracle? To whom or what does one attribute it? To our religious affinity? To yours? The fact is that all the children could have easily opted for violence or nihilism, but you directed us toward confidence and reconciliation. You supported and encouraged us to put stake in the future and the community. Your book demonstrates this. I love what you say about their family lives: the spouse of this one, the children of another. . . .

I have kept in touch with a few of them. We often recall the time we spent at Ambloy and Taverny. We speak of you, Judith, and Niny and the other instructors. When I meet former members of the homes during my trips, I take them aside and we talk and talk.

I am happy that you wrote this book, Judith. It is a grave and upsetting matter; nevertheless, it makes me laugh now and then.

I hope you know what role you have played in our existence.

Elie Wiesel

Introduction

One summer day in 1945, a photograph taken in the port
of Haifa was published in *Haaretz*, an Israeli newspaper. It
showed a little, eight-year-old boy standing next to a travel
bag, pointing a hunting gun at the passengers. He was one
of the children who had been liberated from Buchenwald
by the American soldiers. Lulek was waiting for his brother,
Naphtali, who had left to fetch the rest of their luggage
from customs, and he was going to kill, with his toy gun,
anybody who tried to take away his bag. When a man
carrying a camera—an object he had never seen before—
approached him, he started shooting at him, convinced that
the man was going to steal his belongings.

An eight-year-old survivor of Buchenwald? Yes. One and
a half million babies and children died in the camps, but
several hundreds were saved. I was head of one of the homes
rented by the O.S.E. and closely followed their return to
normal life. As one of them said after growing up, the time
he spent in the children's home had been a period of transition, spanning a bridge between the camps and a new life.
The past experiences of these children created an extremely
delicate situation with which we had to deal. I shall talk
about this period in the first part of this book, and will
devote the second part to the statements given by the children after they had become adults. These statements were
rendered sparingly, for talking about the camps stirred up
terrible memories.

I owe thanks to all of those who have talked, and to their
families, a great many of whom had not known about their
husband's or father's past until these interviews were granted.

11

Chapter One

From Auschwitz to Liberation

On April 11, 1945, the American troops arrived at Buchenwald. When these war-hardened men, who had been prepared to die and to kill, set their eyes on the largest place of death in the world, they were petrified and shocked. Thousands of weak men heaped together in cots were just waiting to join the piles of skeletons outside. The soldiers went from barracks to barracks until they reached number 66. What they saw there struck them with horror: hundreds of skeleton-like children, all boys, silently looking at them with huge, deeply set eyes, their faces resembling those of old men. They were Hungarian and Polish children ranging in age from eight to twenty.

The commander of the American troops was totally bewildered and sent a cable to the O.S.E. in Geneva: "Have found a thousand Jewish children in Buchenwald. Take immediate measures to evacuate them."

At that time I was a refugee in Geneva, working at the O.S.E., and made efforts to obtain visas for the children. Two hundred and eighty visas were issued by Switzerland, 480 by France, and 250 by England; the children would be leaving Buchenwald in June.

In the meantime, the American troops provided for the youngsters most urgent needs—food and clothing. All of the children wore dreadful striped pajamas which were too large in most cases; but by a horrible twist of fate, the only replacements the Americans could find were the uniforms of the Hitler Youth.

The soldiers overdid their kindness and stuffed the youngsters with oversized cans of food, sweets, and chewing gum, and, consequently, many of the children died of overeating. Typhus swept through the camp and the only remedy was to cover the poor, little, fever-burning bodies with constantly renewed, fresh sheets.

These children had lived through the very deepest misery that one could imagine. They were first taken to Auschwitz where they had been treated like adults. They rose between 4:00 and 5:00 in the morning and were given thirty minutes to wash (each barracks had only a few faucets) and to straighten up their cots. Next came roll-call, conducted for one hour in the open air, regardless of the weather. The children had to form in rows of five to march off to work, to rejoin the digging, transportation, quarry, mine, and welding groups. Their hard work was accompanied by the harassments and blows of the guards.

Newcomers repeatedly attempted to escape from their work teams or tried to join other, less harsh ones. They were always caught and heavily punished, or were gassed when judged unable to work. They soon realized that it was best not to attract attention, to vanish in the crowds.

They were not allowed to rest at all during the day; when night came, they again formed in rows of five and returned to camp. Despite the fact that they were totally exhausted, the SS forced them to pass in front of an orchestra formed of other prisoners playing merry martial tunes and to line up once more in the camp's central court for a second roll-call, the terror of every prisoner. Between 60,000 and 70,000 prisoners had to stand at attention, hour upon hour, under the fierce glare of the search-lights, come wind or snow, in 20 degrees below zero or in the smoldering heat, while the SS called out their numbers. If a single man was missing, no one was allowed to move until he was found. The prisoners often fell to the ground in exhaustion, snow covering their bodies. They were going to die, but none of their comrades could help them. Whether dead or alive, a prisoner had to appear at roll-call. If one of them died during work, his companions dragged his body during the long march back to camp in order that he might be there.

After the never-ending ordeal, the prisoners returned to their barracks to be handed their daily food ration: a bowl of a somewhat clear soup, a small piece of margarine and a small loaf of bread, part of which they hid in their pockets or under their pillows for the following morning. They drank a coffee substitute without milk or sugar, which could not give them the strength they needed to accomplish hard labor. Under these circumstances, the prisoners quickly lost weight. Those who lacked resistance or had withered organs were unable to function and were unfit for work. They were called the "Moslems," and the children shied away from them for fear of being infected by their despair and apathy, knowing that all "Moslems" ended up in the gas chambers.

All of the children worked very hard, with the exception of two small boys who had arrived at Auschwitz at ages five and six. They looked much smaller, though, for their life in the ghettos had stunted their growth. Their fathers succeeded in hiding them in their blocks, saving their own food rations for them. The boys' fathers died in camp.

The children of barracks 66 were quick to adapt to life in the camp; their ability to adapt greatly contributed to their survival. The youngest children reacted best because they realized that united they were strong. In many cases they helped their elders, supporting them and taking over responsibilities. The children who, upon their arrival, were placed in the same groups as their brothers or cousins, made every possible effort not to be separated from them, neither in the barracks nor during work. Those without parents in the camp searched for a comrade, a companion. Without one, the hard struggle of everyday life would have been unbearable—mutual moral support being the last and only resort of human fraternity.

Due to the imminent arrival of the Soviets, Auschwitz was evacuated in January 1945 and 61,000 prisoners were pushed towards the west. Week after week they moved along on foot through the cold and the snow, clad only in rags and without food. Once in a while they were permitted to sleep for a few hours along the side of the road, but most of the time they continued marching as if hypnotized. Those unable to move on were shot.

The children retained the horrible memory of this exodus. Upon their arrival in France, all they could speak of was this "evacuation," the atrocities of which surpassed all those of Auschwitz and Buchenwald.

At the beginning of March, 1945, between 10,000 and 12,000 of those who had survived the march arrived in Buchenwald, situated near the city of Weimar, Germany. But the nightmare had not ended. Food rations were even smaller than than they had been in Auschwitz. Fourty-seven thousand prisoners lived in Buchenwald. When the American troops closed in to liberate the camp, the Nazis shot a great number of prisoners in the nearby forest and herded 26,000 persons, most of them Jews, into fifty railroad cars heading for Dachau, near Munich. All of those aboard the train died of hunger, cold, or asphyxiation.

The children who came to France were the survivors of this genocide. Surprisingly, not a single act of vengeance was committed against German civilians during their brief stay in Germany. The children told us that many prisoners went to German houses and asked for food. One of them asked for a violin to play Hungarian music, another for a camera to take pictures of Buchenwald. Some of the young people stole chickens in Weimar, others stole bicycles or motorcycles. To them this was not theft; they considered it their due, a sort of compensation.

When they wanted to take their "treasures" along to France, the person in charge of the convoy discouraged them, promising that in France they would find an abundance of everything. All of them obeyed except for David, who would not leave his violin behind. Yet, in France, people were just as short of goods.

The children were completely bewildered after liberation. They had no families left and had no idea of what the future would bring. After the Yalta agreements, their home countries, Poland and Hungary, had vanished behind the iron curtain. Many of the prisoners in Buchenwald had been German communists, deported because of their political adherence. They had tried to indoctrinate the young people of barracks 66, urging them to return to their countries in order to help the new government, but the children distrusted them, realizing that they would lose their freedom once again. What most of them really wanted to do was to leave for Palestine, the country of the Jews; but Israel was under British mandate and would not admit them, so they decided to accept the proposition of the O.S.E. to go to a free country of Western Europe—Switzerland, France, or England.

Chapter Two

Arrival in France

The special French train arrived in Buchenwald on June 2, 1945, and the children stormed it for fear that it would leave without them. Dr. Revel, who accompanied the children, said that "dressed in their striped pajamas or in uniforms of the Hitler Youth, they looked like young savages." Unable to remember their names after having been addressed only by their numbers or nicknames, many of them suffered an identity crisis.

Each time the train stopped, the boys jumped out to pillage the countryside, but once in France, these acts of vandalism stopped. Another problem soon arose, however. After seeing the German uniforms, the French population thought the boys to be enemies and attacked the train. At the Metz railroad station, the children were in such great danger that the train had to be pushed onto a side track overnight, and the words "K.L. (Concentration Camp) Buchenwald—Orphans" were painted on the cars. The convoy took four days to arrive at Ecouis in Normandy, as the conductor had been instructed to stop the train whenever some of the boys jumped off to run through the countryside.

Ecouis was a converted sanitarium that the French Government had put at the disposal of the O.S.E. The director of Ecouis had prepared 500 little beds unaware that 440 adolescents between the ages of 12 and 21 would arrive; only 30 of them were between eight and 12 years old. They looked like a group of bandits: they were suspicious and mute, their heads shorn, their faces swollen from hunger;

19

not a smile showed on any of their faces. They were apathetic towards the outside world. Their eyes spoke of sadness and suspicion, for the supervisors of the home seemed to be no better than the guards of the camps. But most of all, they were terrorized by the sight of the doctors, who must have reminded them of Dr. Mengele—the man who had awaited their arrival in Auschwitz, sending the feeble ones to the gas chambers and selecting the able-bodied for slave labor.

The children of Ecouis were convinced that everything was owed to them after many years of deprivation. The food that the American soldiers had given them was of much better quality than what France could offer during that first year after the war. The boys were able to obtain additional food from nearby farms by trading blankets, sheets, dishes and pots from the home. One of them, now a jeweller of excellent reputation, stole little dogs which he sold in Paris.

Victor, an adolescent of 15 who looked much younger, decided to go to Paris with a friend. He had heard about an underground train and a rescue center, the Hotel Lutetia, where survivors of camps could go for help. The two boys hitchhiked to Paris on a truck carrying sand, but the closer the truck came to Paris, the more frightened they became. Neither of them spoke a word of French and they had never seen a big city. When the driver left them off at nighttime, they walked until they came to steps leading underground. "Let's go," said Victor. "This must be the underground train."

Once underground, they asked for the "Hotel Lutetia." The answer they received was "Sevres-Babylone." Victor, who had learned a few words of English from the American soldiers, understood "Sevres" to mean "seven." "Babylone" could only be a stop since they were in a station, so they counted seven stops and got out, thinking that they had arrived. Once on the street, they again asked for the "Hotel Lutetia," but couldn't understand a word of the long explanation they were given. At last, someone walked them the long distance to the Hotel Lutetia, a huge and absolutely fabulous building. They marvelled at the large room with twin beds, but most of all, at the white telephone that they could not keep from touching.

Suddenly, there was a knock at the door, and a priest, Abbé Glasberg, a Jew of Polish descent, entered the room. He had helped many Jews during the war, and spoke Polish and Yiddish (a mixture of German and Hebrew, spoken by the Jews in Eastern Europe). They started talking, and on the following day the priest put the two friends on a train for Ecouis. When they arrived home they told their eagerly listening comrades: "Paris is a wonderful city. There are huge hotels with large beds and white telephones and all the priests speak Polish and Yiddish."

In later years, Victor settled in Paris and became an electronic engineer. According to him, it was the white telephone at the Hotel Lutetia that led him to choose his profession.

The architecture of Ecouis, unfortunately, reminded the children of the camps. In addition, the director spoke only French and German and could communicate only with the Rumanians who knew a little French. All the other boys showed no reaction whatsoever when addressed in German. When pieces of bread were handed out, memories of the camps returned to the boys, and they requested that the bread be put on the table so that they could help themselves to it. At the end of each meal the leftovers disappeared into their rooms as one could never be sure when the next meal would be served.

For these young people, all adults were potential enemies who were not to be trusted. One day we served them Camembert after a meal and the strong smell convinced them that they were being poisoned; they threw the Camembert at the adults' heads. The French courses organized by the director were not very successful either. The children had the impression that they were being enticed to settle in France and the idea did not appeal to them. France was too close to Germany; all they wanted was to leave for Palestine. England issued fifty visas for the group living in Ecouis, promising more for the future, but the promise was not kept.

From the very beginning, Hungarians and Poles were divided into two distinct groups, violently fighting each

21

other—a carry-over from the camps, where the last ones to arrive thought the other inmates to be privileged. The personnel were unable to understand their motives or to conceive of what the children had been through, as they talked about the camps only among themselves.

Many visitors came to Ecouis to talk with the young survivors of Buchenwald. The boys just sat silently, listening to the beautiful and affectionate words, but showing no reactions, as they were totally disillusioned about human nature.

One day an American army chaplain, Chaplain Marcus, came to Ecouis. He had met the boys before in Buchenwald. They sat in a circle around him on the lawn. The chaplain stood in front of them unable to utter a word, as tears of emotion filled his eyes. It had been a long time since the children had seen an adult cry; freed from an inner tension they, too, started crying. Later, one of the boys told us: "The chaplain had revived our souls and revealed the deeply buried feelings within us."

After this incident, many family memories which had been repressed since life in camp, came back to the boys. Most of the children came from large, devout families, that respected rest on Sabbath, did not eat pork or impure meats (only Kosher food), and scrupulously followed daily prayers. These memories prompted them to a decision which helped many of them to regain their identity. They chose a Jewish instructor as a spokesman, Leo Margulies, who had spent six years in Buchenwald and strictly observed Jewish traditions. The boys trusted him because of his strong charisma. Mr. Margulies requested that Kosher food be served but the director of the home was totally dismayed by his request; to observe the rules of Kosher cooking for 500 persons was impossible due to the difficult circumstances of 1945. Mr. Margulies therefore suggested that a smaller home be opened for those who wanted to abide by the rules of Jewish religion and the O.S.E. agreed.

Consequently, about one hundred children and adolescents were transferred to the beautiful castle of Ambloy, near the town of Vendome; it was surrounded by a huge park, forests and a lake. It was there that I met the children

22

of Buchenwald. I had just returned to France where I had been living before the war. My father had not returned from Auschwitz and the rest of my family was dispersed throughout the world. While in Geneva, I had heard about the existence of the children of Buchenwald and had decided to visit them. I sat on the lawn with them, watching their stern faces; they, apparently, did not notice my presence. They spoke in Yiddish about the camps, the evacuation from Auschwitz, the long march to Buchenwald, and the last day in barracks 66.

The director of Ambloy was upset about the boys' aggressiveness towards him. Like most directors of homes for survivors of Buchenwald (called "B homes"), he believed that they were true psychopaths, cold and indifferent by nature, and that this was the reason why they were able to survive camplife.

The day after my arrival was a Friday, the beginning of Sabbath, which was celebrated by a special dinner. The boys started singing religious songs, their faces still stern and cold, but I was deeply moved by their fervent voices and realized that these were not indifferent faces, but ones marked by the indescribable sufferings of the past. I decided to stay at Ambloy, and when the director left, I took over the home with Niny, a young counselor from Ecouis.

Niny and I understood that all traditional methods of education were bound to fail; we had to be practical and adapt to the boys' condition. But what could be achieved by observing them and showing our affection if we could not communicate with them? We only spoke German, the language of their tormentors, and definitely could not use it, so we learned Yiddish by listening to their conversations; even though we did not learn to speak it well, it was much better than German. We also decided to find out their names for we certainly could not call them by their numbers. It took a tremendous effort to discover the identity of each, as they all looked alike at first sight. Sitting together on the lawn, or during meals, we would ask them over and over again: "What is your name?" Once we were able to say, "Hello, Moshe Cohen!" or "How are you, Abraham Weiss?", the

23

boys would remain silent at first, but a shy smile would slowly appear on their faces. Their identity had been restored to them, and this was the beginning of communication.

As I have already mentioned, fights between Hungarians and Poles persisted in Ambloy. Each morning I would watch the injured line up at the infirmary. I would ask them the reasons for their quarrel and would not take care of them unless they had first made peace.

Because of what we had learned about life in the camps, we realized how artificial the organization of the home (such as the division of dormitories into age groups) must have seemed to them. We therefore told them that they were free to chose their roommates, and they formed groups of various sizes based on their home towns. The large dormitories were filled with survivors of Cluj, Munkacs, Oradia Mare, and other towns, while the smaller rooms were occupied by the Polish survivors from Lodz and Pietrkow. The boys wrote the names of their home towns on the bedroom doors.

Each group consisted of boys ranging from eight to 21 years of age, the older ones taking care of the children. Little by little the fighting came to an end. Whenever a quarrel started, the friends of the antagonists would intervene and stop the disputes. A fraternal atmosphere soon developed, not only in the individual rooms, but throughout the whole group.

In order to discontinue the habit of hoarding food in their bedrooms, we decided to leave the kitchen doors open and told the boys that they were free to help themselves to bread, cookies, eggs and jam. This meant extra work for Niny and myself, as we had to collect plates and dishes throughout the house. "This is your home; everything is at your disposal," we often told them. "There is no need to take leftovers to your rooms." Food was still the most important issue and the boys were very grateful for our efforts to obtain Kosher meat. They kept us company in the kitchen, "just like home," and stopped acting like squirrels.

All children and adolescents adore looking at photos of

themselves and our boys were no exception; they often went to Vendôme by themselves just to have their pictures taken. We asked the S.N.C.F. (French Railroad Company) to add a special car to the Thursday train, and after the weekly session at the municipal bath house, we would all go to the photographer who must have made the business of his life with us.

Due to the freedom and trust the children enjoyed and the religious practices observed by us, an harmonious atmosphere spread throughout the house. The young people seemed to settle down and to open up, revealing to us a subtle image of their pre-war faces.

Yet, their mentality basically had not changed. They kept talking about the camps and went over the lists of survivors, searching for members of their families. The chances of finding any of them diminished each day, but some of the boys persisted in their hope. On Yom Kippur, the day of atonement, cruel reality emerged. When saying the Kadish, the prayer for the dead, they engaged in passionate discussions and disputes. Some refused to say the prayer for their parents, brothers and sisters: "They might not be dead. How awful and disgraceful to pray for them as if they were dead!" Others retorted: "But you have been in Auschwitz yourself; you have seen the gas chambers with your own eyes, the smoke, the corpses. You witnessed what happened to the women and children. Why keep any illusions? We have to say the prayers for the dead!" In the end, some of them left the synagogue while others continued to say the prayers.

All of those I later met again remembered this day of Yom Kippur for it had marked a turning point in their lives. From that day on, memories of their families came back to them. It may be just a coincidence, but those who had left the synagogue refusing to admit the deaths of their relatives, later married French or American women, or Israeli women who had spent all of their lives in Israel. They buried their past deep within themselves and never talked about the camps.

Those who had said Kadish later married former inmates

25

of camps, or young women who had lived in Europe during the war. They had felt the desire to speak about the camps to their children but lacked the courage.

During the months in Ambloy and Taverny (I shall write about Taverny later in this book), our main objective was to restore the boys' faith in humanity and in themselves. However, we could hardly perceive the distress of their concentration camp life. I am therefore rendering the account of Lulek, the little boy in the photograph mentioned in the book's introduction.

Lulek is a diminutive of Israel, Israel Lau. Despite his young age, he has become High Priest of Natanya (Israel). Lulek has become very popular through radio and television, especially among the young generation. He has recently published a very dynamic and frank book about Judaism in everyday life. A tall and well-groomed man who speaks an extremely polished Hebrew, Lulek is married to the daughter of a well-known rabbi and has eight children:

> *I was born twice; therefore, I have a better view of things. Of course, biologically, I was born only once, but spiritually, my birth was twofold: first in June, 1937, in Pietrkow, and then when I arrived in the Holy Land on July 17, 1945, the day of Ticha Beav.[1] I was eight years old then. I speak about a second birth because it is hard to conceive that after the experiences of Buchenwald, of the long way covered in convoys and on the roads, of the hideouts and the cold, that such a little orphan eventually developed into a little boy wearing blue and white shorts, playing soccer and tossing marbles. I had walked among the dead and had helped push the carts piled with corpses to the crematory. Still, the same little boy had learned to sing again: "Ouga, ouga, ouga,"[2] and to recite the alphabet. Could I actually be the same person?*
>
> *When I arrived in Israel, it seemed as if a barrier stood between me and the other people. I only knew one*

[1] Day of fasting, commemorating the destruction of the first and second Temples of Jerusalem, and announcing the exile.
[2] Children's counting rhyme, meaning "cake, cake, cake."

26

person, my brother Naphtali; (his story will follow later in this book) he had arrived here with me and, of course, I did not want to leave him. . . .

When I asked him if he wanted to tell me more about himself, he responded negatively:

No, I don't want to continue my story. At all types of ceremonies I talk about the deported people, about their sufferings and their experiences, but in general terms only. I never reveal anything about myself. . . I cannot. . . . After Buchenwald was liberated, several people wanted to take me with them. My brother Naphtali spoke about the Holy Land, which didn't mean a thing to me. I couldn't speak a word of Hebrew or Yiddish, only Polish and a few words of Russian and German. A Russian officer called Fiedor was determined to adopt me and to take me with him to Russia. He was so full of life and in much better health than Naphtali, who, at age 19, was a real "Moslem." After liberation, I saw Fiedor ride a horse without using a saddle at such a frightening speed that it left me in awe. In Buchenwald he had stolen some pieces of wool and knitted earmuffs for me. When the Germans yelled "Mützeab!" ("Hats off!") at roll-call and assembly, my ears stayed nice and warm.

There was also a Frenchman, I believe he was a doctor, who also wanted to adopt me. He described the beauty of France and Paris to me. At the time of liberation, I contracted chicken-pox and was put in quarantine on the second floor of the infirmary. My brother found a ladder, climbed through the window, wrapped me in a sheet, and took me down to line up for registration to join the Alya of the young.[1] They only had a few places available, and had we missed this opportunity, we would have had to remain in Germany for several years. I stood in line and signed with my thumb print, as I didn't know how to write. My brother kept telling me that

[1]An organization taking care of Jewish children who wanted to emigrate to Palestine.

27

Palestine was a marvellous country, where only Jews lived and where we would be able to lead a wonderful life.

Upon our arrival in Haifa, about 200 young people were standing on the bridge of the ship, admiring Carmel and the bay of Haifa. We saw Arabs working in the port, wearing pants as large as bags. I had seen all kinds of uniforms, but never any pants of this size, and I asked a kind Jewish man why these men were wearing such funny pants. Not thinking that I was still a child, he answered: "They aren't Jews, they are Arabs. They wear those large pants in order to hide the children they have stolen, and they sell them on the market as slaves." I promptly retorted: "Ich gehe nicht! ("I won't go!") I didn't come here to be stolen and sold on the market. I won't leave the ship!"

At the rescue center of Atlit, we were put behind fences once again, and we stayed there for two weeks. Our names had been published in all of the newspapers, and many people came to ask for news about their families who had remained in Europe. Thousands of people stood outside of the fences and called out names: "Eisenberg from Lodz," and so forth. One day in August, a very tall, young man wearing khaki clothing, sandals, and a cap on his blond hair arrived at the center. Naphtali exclaimed: "Lulek, there's your brother!" It was Chiko. When the war started, he had been studying in a yeshiva in Rumania. Since then, we were without news from him and feared the worst. But he had managed to escape and had come to Palestine in 1944. He was a member of the Kibbutz Kfar Etzion, where some of the members had seen our names in the newspapers. Chiko, who was working in the fields at that time, dropped everything to come see us.

Two weeks later, several busses picked us up from Atlit and took us to various parts of the country according to our political beliefs. In our case, of course, since I was so young, we went to the part of the country that corresponded to Naphtali's beliefs. We were sent to a children's home in Kfar-Saba and had to live in bar-racks once more for about one month. An uncle, a former rabbi of Katovice, Poland, found us there.

Upon his arrival in the Holy Land in 1940 with his wife and daughter, my uncle had nothing to call his own. He had become a rabbi in a small town near Haifa. He was a handsome, well-dressed man, with a beautiful grey beard à la Hertzl; he gave me chocolate and socks for a present. He and Naphtali engaged in a long discussion behind closed doors during which they decided that it wasn't proper for a little boy of eight to be dragged from one home to another. Having only one daughter, 12 years of age, my uncle agreed to take me in while Naphtali attended a yeshiva at Petáh-Tikva. Naphtali had not told me his plans because he knew that I didn't trust a soul. The only thing he said to me was: "Let's go and visit our uncle; he lives in a town where people live in straw huts because they are very poor, except for our uncle, who, being a rabbi, owns a beautiful wooden house."

This was his way to prepare me psychologically. When we arrived at my uncle's beautiful house, I was very impressed by the blue tiles in the staircase. My aunt, my mother's sister, opened the door; deeply moved, she kissed me and spoke to me in Polish. At least we had a common language. She had set a beautiful table and had put chocolate cigarettes on a plate just for me, but I declined and said very seriously: "No, thank you, I don't smoke." Naphtali stayed for three days. Then he explained: "Well, I'll be leaving for the yeshiva and you are going to stay here." I cried bitterly—nothing was going to make me stay behind—but it was to no avail. I had to get used to the idea of living with my relatives.

When accompanying my aunt to the grocery store, I clutched her hand for fear that she might abandon me. All the neighbors knew my story, felt sorry for me and tried to be nice to me. But I kept my distance.

Two boys, Ygal and Ouri, lived in the only two-story house on our street. They wanted to play with me, but I *was not very cooperative. I was quite short; I could walk under a table without bending over. When I was in the yard one day, one of the two boys, who was older than me, brought out a big, beautiful red ball. He spoke Hebrew, I spoke Polish; the ball was to be, in a way, our common tongue. But I did not want to catch it. I had never played with a ball and I was suspicious. He wouldn't give up, though, and when I finally agreed to catch the ball, I went towards him, and standing on tiptoe, pinched his cheek as if to say "you are a nice boy."*

When school started again, I found myself enrolled in first grade even though I was already eight years old. But I could not speak Hebrew. On our first day, we learned only one word: "shalom" (hello, peace); shalom dad, shalom mom. As noontime approached, a boat was drawn on the blackboard in honor of the new emigrant—myself: there were plenty of heads on the deck and the whole class shouted "shalom!" I went home to my aunt and said: "I'm not going back to school. The teachers make us sit for four hours just to learn one word. That's nothing for me." My aunt went to see the principal and he told her: "When he can count to 20 in Hebrew and understand what 'more' and 'less' mean, then he can be admitted into second grade." My aunt taught all of that to me the very same day, and the next day I was admitted into second grade. A month later, I knew enough Hebrew to go into third grade and be with children my own age. But I found the daily routine of school, so different from what I had known until then, to be unbearable. I had entered third grade four months before the end of school year. For the annual awards ceremony, the pupils made a cart used to bring in the harvest; it was for me, who had harvested so many grades in just one year.

Lulek was not like other children. Instead of feeling sorry for himself, he tried to surround himself with an air of glory in order to impress his friends:

*In Buchenwald, the prisoners' numbers were not tat-
tooed on their arms but sewn into their shirt sleeves. I
was very humiliated when I found out that other deported
persons wore tattoos. Nobody was going to believe that I
had been in a camp! So, I wrote my number on my arm
with ink but it disappeared after the first bath. My pride
was restored on another occasion, however: the government had decided to give a general vaccination against
typhus or smallpox, I don't remember which. Since this
was very costly, they initially gave a slight vaccination. If
a swelling appeared it meant that the body had had this
sickness or a more serious one. I implored God to make
my arm swell, and it did! I was immune; I had been
through great ordeals!*

*I had never talked about the camps to my friends
before, but at this point they realized that I was different
from them.*

*Another event comes to mind. Even though I ignored
the date of my parents' death, I joined those families
who said Kadish on the 10th of Tevet,[1] a date established
by the rabbi as the day of collective mourning. At the
end of worship, the son saying Kadish has to distribute
liquors, cognac and cookies in order to celebrate the
ascension of the souls. Since I wasn't able to do that, I
did something else. The grocer had given me a large,
empty cookie box where I stored the marbles that I had
won. Being 13 years old, I decided that it was about time
for me to be morally prepared for life at the yeshiva and
that I wasn't going to continue playing with marbles
like a baby. On the 10th of Tevet, I distributed all my
marbles at school, explaining the reasons for my gen-
erosity. It was a rather unusual way to celebrate the
ascension of my parents' souls. . . .*

I asked Lulek if he had talked to others about the camps.
He said:

---

[1]Fasting for the commemoration of the siege of Jerusalem by Nebuchadnezzar.

31

I didn't mention the camps, not even to my uncle. The first time I talked in front of others was during the Eichmann trial. I was staying with my in-laws at the time; we listened to the radio broadcast of the trial, the testimonies of witnesses and Hausner's speech for the prosecution: "I am representing six million victims." As a former deported person, my brother, Naphtali, had been sent to the trial as a reporter for the newspaper Haaretz. He, however, could not bear the pressure and left Jerusalem to stay with us in an attempt to find relief. We exchanged memories about the camps—an unusual thing for us to do.

Since I am a rabbi I am often invited to different communities' commemorations for 27 Nissan, the official day for "Deportation and Bravery," and for 10 Tevet. Instead of beginning with the chant "El Male Rá hamin" (God of Mercy), I usually ask for the commemoration book of the community and read a few excerpts. When I talk in schools, children are quick to realize that I am not just speaking as a rabbi, but that I am personally involved. I usually not only relate the facts that everybody is aware of by now, but I also talk about the emotions they stir up. I refuse to accept the tribute paid to the insurgents' bravery and courage, as if the others had not also been heroes.

In the evenings, my father-in-law would read a chapter about a community which disappeared in order to accomplish the commandment of the Torah: "Remember Amalek."[1] He is an extraordinary man who I met at the yeshiva long before he became my father-in-law. The first time I saw his daughter in Bne-Bray, I decided to marry her, but didn't call on her father then. I did not meet her again for six months; then, after having found work at my old yeshiva in Jerusalem, I called her brother, explaining to him that while I knew that the father usually made the request for his son, I could not abide by

[1]Deut.XV, 17. The people of Amalek attacked the people of Israel in the desert, beginning with the sick and feeble ones. Amalek represents the evil no one should ever forget.

*the custom for I was an orphan. I was finally permitted
to make a date with the young girl; we saw each other
frequently and secretly became engaged. I still hadn't
seen her father, the rabbi, but in the end he agreed to see
me at his house on a Saturday evening after Sabbath.*

*He was alone and served me an excellent dinner.
Then he spoke to me: "After three sons God blessed us
with a girl. My wife and I love her dearly. I was told that
you are a very talented student, but I must be honest
with you and will explain the reasons why I hesitated to
give my only daughter to a man who is alone in the
world, who never had a family life and does not remember his parents. How can such a man raise a family?
Will he make our daughter happy? I would like to cite a
verse of the Torah: 'For this (marriage), a man will leave
his father and mother . . . ' (Gen.XX, 24). I won't translate
the word 'azav' literally with 'leave,' but rather with the
word 'izavon,' which has the same root and meaning as
'heritage.' I believe that because of her education, our
daughter has what is needed to create the basis for a
solid and genuine Jewish family, and I trust you to make
her happy." From that day on my life has been different.
I am received like a son in the rabbi's family and my
wife and I now have eight children.*

Let us now return to Ambloy where the summer neared
its end. As a whole, the group seemed to feel much better
than it did at its arrival, but some of the boys suffered deep
depressions. One evening, on the way to my room, I came
across a tall, very thin young man with large, soft eyes. I
had never seen him before! It was about three o'clock in the
morning; he was leaning out of the window looking at the
beautiful trees in the park. I asked him his name: "I do not
exist," he answered, "I don't want to live anymore. I don't
want to see the sun, nor daylight ever again. I only get up at
nighttime to smell the wind."

I wondered how he managed to get food.

"My comrades bring me food, but I won't live much
longer. Each day brings me closer to death."

33

I talked to him several nights in a row and little by little I found out about his childhood. He had been living in Sotmar in a warm family atmosphere. He had two elder sisters and had been the only son for a long time. Later, four younger brothers and sisters were born.

It took him a long time to get interested in life again and he did not leave his room until it was time to depart from Ambloy. He learned his father's trade—printing—and is now living in Brooklyn, one of the Jewish sections of New York. He is married and has several children.

One of the most severe cases was Aron, who tried several times to jump out of the window of his room. We put him into a room on the ground floor, but this did not solve his problems. He refused to talk for many weeks. Because of his physical strength, he had been working in one of the "Sonderkommandos" of Auschwitz. These commandoes were in charge of carting the bodies to the crematories. He had also been compelled to transport the bodies of his dead parents and "hadn't felt anything;" now, he cannot forgive himself.

Aron lives in Israel today. He remembers having suffered from a depression in Ambloy, but ignores what caused it.

The sense of culpability of Zoltan was of a different nature and showed other effects. He was terribly thin and desperately tried to gain weight, but had to vomit whatever he swallowed. Before deportation he had been in love with a young girl, Edna, and they had intended to marry and leave for Israel. His parents, however, disapproved and had engaged him to another girl, Myriam. His parents and Myriam died in concentration camps, leaving Zoltan and Edna. The idea that Myriam's death, in fact, "suited him" was the cause of Zoltan's illness. He physically reacted to his guilt complex by refusing all food, all possibility of survival.

Once his problem was analyzed, Zoltan was able to eat normally again. He was one of the first to leave for Israel— where Edna had just married.

Only two of our boys actually made plans for their future. They had asked to share a room, even though one was Polish and the other Hungarian, and they prepared for the university together. One of them was Kalman Kalikstein, a noted nuclear scientist in the United States and a professor at New York University. The other was Eli Wiesel, the famous author, whose works give evidence of the holocaust. He wrote his first book, *The Night*, in a notebook at Ambloy.

The O.S.E. considered Ambloy a sort of recovery home and the time had come to think about the future, to take a realistic view and to prepare for the children's integration into society. After Yom-Kippur we asked each of the boys their intentions for the future. The youngest ones, who did not read or write, would have to go to school, but this prospect scared them. The idea of being separated from the group, of having to mingle with other children, was frightening. Would they be accepted by others? Twelve-year-old Jankel said to me: "Judith, please, I'll do whatever you want, but don't send me to school, I couldn't stand it!" The O.S.E. helped us resolve the problem by creating a special class for the smallest ones.

At our question, "What do you want to learn?" the adolescents looked at Niny and me in complete bewilderment. They did not know; they did not want anything. We therefore took a different approach, inquiring about their fathers' trades. Many of them welcomed the idea of carrying on tradition and reviving their past, and decided to learn their father's trade, be it furrier, tailor, leather-maker, or watchmaker.

35

Chapter Three

At the Crossroads: Taverny

Halfway between Paris and Enghien, the train stopped at the little station of Vaucelles. The Castle of Vaucelles, a large property lying in the middle of a park, was to be the new home for the boys, Niny, and myself. It had been requisitioned by the Germans during the war. Our first chore was to remove the heavy iron gate which they had erected for protection.

The boys were free to decide which dormitory or room they wanted to move into and who they wanted to sit with in the dining room. During the two years in Taverny, none of them changed their initial seating places. Recently, I met a "former child of Taverny" and was able to describe the place he had occupied in the dining room; he exclaimed, "Of course, it was the one closest to the kitchen!"

The younger ones were sent to Jewish Vocational School, the O.R.T., then located in the Rue des Saules near Montmartre. I once had to go to Paris on an errand and was among the latecomers. The train had already started to move and some of the boys raced after it, trying to jump on. I was terrified watching them fall to the ground and thought the train had run over them; I fainted from shock when I saw them get back to their feet. They had to carry me home. When the other boys returned that evening, all of them came to see me in my room. They were overwhelmed because I was concerned of their fate to the point of fainting, actually falling ill at the idea that something could have happened to them.

In addition to their studies and schooling, the boys helped with the chores in the house and prepared Shabbat. The little ones of the O.S.E. school also pitched in for they wanted to be with their "brothers." Together, we prepared for the Jewish holidays, each boy having a specific function to accomplish.

The two oldest boys led the Jewish life in the spirit of the former congregations. Myer-Tzvi, who descended from a line of marvellous rabbis, was the spiritual head and was followed by everyone. Moshe, a strong and healthy boy and a leader of men, prepared worship ceremonies. He felt responsible for the religious behavior of his comrades.

I had been absent during one Shabbat and when I returned home Sunday morning, I sensed an unusual tension throughout the house. The boys told me what had happened: as usual, a warm and peaceful atmosphere had spread over the house, when suddenly Shlomo walked in dressed in work clothes. There was no doubt that he had taken the train from Paris even though travelling was forbidden during Shabbat. All heads turned towards him and Moshe silently stood up, walked over to Shlomo and slapped his face. Niny, who deeply disapproved of such repressive methods, left the room without saying a word. The joy of Shabbat had been shattered.

The directors of other "B" homes in Ecouis, also housing "Buchenwald children," had been selected according to their sense of authority. They envied us for they could not understand why our liberal methods were so successful. But Simon found the religious life of Vaucelles far too strict, and on a Monday morning decided to go to another "B" home in Le Vésinet. He was back by Tuesday evening, though, and we accepted him without asking questions.

Twenty years later I happened to meet the former director of Le Vésinet. When he learned that Simon was now living in the United States with his family, he exclaimed: "That's impossible! The boy is crazy and must make his family very unhappy. He arrived at Le Vésinet one evening at nine o'clock and declared, 'I am hungry.' I told him that, unfortunately, dinner in our house was served at seven o'clock and that the next meal would be breakfast. He replied, 'But I told you that I am hungry now! Don't you understand?' I quietly explained to him that we were running an orderly house, that everything was cleared away after meals and that he could not eat before the next morning. He stormed into the kitchen, breaking the locked kitchen door with his shoulders. He opened the cupboards and, like a maniac, threw all the dishes onto the floor."

We were very fortunate to have the help of such outstanding people as Michel and Mr. Margulies. The latter had been a leader of the Jewish Youth Organization and was deported to Buchenwald in 1939. When the camp was liberated, he insisted on being in charge of the children of barracks 66, accompanying them on their journey to France. They trusted and admired him for having survived six years of Buchenwald, and he was on excellent terms with the boys. The O.S.E., however, considering him too old to stay in a children's home, recalled him to Paris. But the children of Ecouis trusted only "Monsieur" Margulies, who had been in camp like them and knew what they had been through, and he was permitted to return. He became their spokesman in all management matters, was an honest and very pious man, and needed to take no drastic measures to have the children accomplish their daily chores.

As for Michel, he arrived one day at Taverny and told us, "My parents were arrested in Paris, but I was able to go into hiding and my life was spared. I am not yet prepared to lead a normal life and would very much like to take care of the young deported children. If you will have me. . . ."

He was about 20 years old at the time and wore shorts and had a crew-cut. His bright eyes and resolute air quickly won the boys' hearts. They were amazed to find out that he was a vegetarian to whom food was not a main issue. He was the only one unharmed when they all suffered from food poisoning after eating spoiled fish, and they wondered whether his was not the true way of life. He was a quiet man, never saying a wrong word. Once he saw the boys pull off the legs of a fly and just asked, "But why?" To this day, the boys remember how deeply ashamed they felt at this question which was bare of any reproach.

Michel had the boys exercise each morning. They were proud of their growing muscles and of the strength returning to their bodies. Being strong, kind, and tolerant, using authority without abusing it, Michel had a very positive influence on the boys and served as an example to them. It helped many of them adjust to the requirements of their new life. Whenever I meet a former inmate of Taverny, his first question is: "Do you know what happened to Michel?" I am able to tell him that Michel is now living in Beer-Sheba, Israel, and is a pacifist, refusing to carry arms. He is still youthful in appearance, wears shorts in summer and winter, has remained a vegetarian and devotes his life to the community.

Israel arrived at Taverny much later. He was 17 years old and had graduated from high school in Israel. He wanted to become a pianist and had registered at the Paris Conservatory, but because of his piano, was unable to find a room. He had heard about us and decided to ask if he could rent a room in Taverny. I offered him the floor above the stables if, in return, he gave a concert for us on Wednesdays.

Israel immediately set to work, replastering and whitewashing the damaged walls of his room. "A Jew has to know all crafts in the Holy Land," he said. When the boys discovered that he was even more talented with the piano than with the trowel, their admiration for him knew no limits. For them, Israel represented the new Jewish generation. They came in great numbers to his Wednesday evening concerts, some of them sitting on the floor, and listened to him talk about Bach's melodies and recurring themes. Then he played for them. The week after, it was Beethoven and his symphonies, then Mozart and his operas. I had bought tickets for the first row of the balcony at the Paris Opera and we went to listen to "The Enchanted Flute." When I saw the childrens' happy and marvelling eyes, I was grateful that destiny had sent Israel to us.

One would have expected that boys of their age, many of them already learning a trade, would feel tempted to leave the home and lead an independent life. Quite the contrary.

Whenever a boy met another survivor from his home country, he would ask him to come to the house, which, in fact, was already quite full. The boys also wanted to invite their friends for Shabbat. The criteria for accepting a boy in Taverny for Shabbat was set by our question: "Do you believe that your parents would have invited him?" Thus, we left the decision to the boys.

On the other hand, we never refused a brother or sister who showed up at Taverny. One day, two young girls clad in rags, their feet wrapped in pieces of cloth, came to Taverny looking for their brother, Icu Gouck. The younger of the two, Lily, gave an account of their journey:

> *After liberation, we returned to our home in Hungary, hoping a member of our family would come back. In November of 1945, we received a telegram from the Red Cross, informing us that our brother, Icu, was living in France. We received a letter from Icu, who was then in Ambloy, and decided to leave for France, illegally crossing the Iron Curtain. We arrived in Paris and, after having found the train for Ambloy, had to travel for many more hours. We dragged ourselves from the station to the home and arrived there late at night. The young girl who opened the door looked at Icu's picture and said, "You are too late. No, don't be afraid, Icu is alive. But he is no longer here—he is in Taverny." She explained to us how to get to Taverny, and we had to spend the night in the waiting room and the station. The next morning at the Gare du Nord, I scrutinized all the passengers and finally showed Icu's picture to a young man wearing a béret. He exclaimed, "I know him well. He lives in the same children's home as I."*

The joy of their reunion was overwhelming. Icu first told them about their father:

> *I was liberated from Buchenwald with Papa, who had survived but was extremely weak. He took me to France on foot and in American trucks. When we arrived at Mulhouse, I was so ill that I had to be taken to a*

41

hospital which had just reopened. The doctors told Papa,
"Your son is about to die. Only a blood transfusion will
save him, but we have no blood reserves." Papa told
them, "Take mine." We were put on two beds, side by
side, and I gained back my strength; I returned to life.
But Papa contracted jaundice and died. After two weeks
in the hospital, not knowing where to go, I returned to
Buchenwald to join my comrades of barracks 66.

The two sisters adjusted very well to life in Taverny. Maggie learned to be a seamstress at the O.R.T. and Lily registered at the Sorbonne. Soon after, two more young girls were brought to Taverny and they, too, took sewing courses at the O.R.T. In no time at all they looked young, healthy and beautiful again. They were admired by all the boys when they came to dinner on Friday evenings in their new, self-made dresses. They had become the sisters of everyone. It was too beautiful to last and, sure enough, one day we received a letter from the O.S.E. in Paris stating: "We have learned that four young girls are living among your boys. This is against the rules. We have reserved four places in one of our homes in Versailles. Organize their immediate transfer."

The girls showed no reaction whatsoever at the news, and one morning I accompanied them to Versailles. Not a word was spoken during the whole trip. The director of Versailles kept me for lunch where I sat across from the four girls. Tears ran down their faces and into their plates during the meal. After dessert, I asked them if they had unpacked. They shook their heads, silently. I then told them, "Go fetch your suitcases, we are returning home."

Many years later the girls admitted to me that leaving Taverny would have meant certain death for them, since they trusted no one.

Maggie and Lily have married camp survivors and are now living in the south of the United States. Lily, with the help of her husband, founded a dress factory. She became an active member of the Jewish community and a frequent guest at women's clubs. But she still felt very lonely, having nothing in common with these women whose concerns seemed futile to her.

A few years ago she finally found the courage to tell her husband about her terrible nightmares, the war memories haunting her dreams. "Since I am unable to talk about it, I think I would like to write a book about what I have been through," Lily said. She and her sister decided to retrace their long journey from their home town to Auschwitz. "I recognized everything; even the odors were still there, unchanged." The two sisters also visited their father's tomb in the old Jewish cemetery of Zillisheim near Mulhouse. They then came to see me in Israel and we talked about Taverny. Upon her return to the United States, Lily published her biography and is now relieved of her terrible burden.

Lily is the mother of four children: two sons, who have made brilliant studies, and a very beautiful daughter who won first prize at a beauty contest in North Carolina. At a press interview she explained, "I entered the contest because my parents had been deported. My mother kept telling me that I would have to live twice: once for myself, and once again to make up for all the things she had missed when she was young."

Nothing could hold the boys back when they learned about a member of their family, generally a brother, that was still alive. They started their search, no matter how far they had to travel. When they returned, discouraged, no one asked any questions, their silent faces speaking for them.

Aron, more or less cured from his depression, was working at the O.R.T. school when he learned that his young brother, Ouri, was living in a children's home in the Black Forest, Germany. He, of course, immediately set off to look for him. After six long weeks he returned and told us what had happened to him:

> *I arrived there, found the home, and recognized my little 12-year-old brother. "Go away!" he yelled. "I don't want to see you, you are dead to me. I became used to the idea that I am left alone in the world, that my parents were dead. Everybody is dead. I don't want to dream any longer."*

Aron left, slept in the open and waited. Around ten o'clock on the following day, the children were taken for a walk. Aron walked alongside Ouri without speaking a word. When Ouri returned to the home, Aron stayed outside. This went on for a month. Then, one morning, Ouri told him, "All right, I accept you, you are alive and you are my brother. Soon we will leave for Eretz Israel. Come join me there." Soon after his return to Taverny, Aron prepared for his departure for Palestine.

The home continued to be a haven of fraternity. Yet, the children were aware that they could not spend the rest of their lives in Taverny and that they would have to overcome their fear of the future and find individual solutions. They often had to go through great trials and tribulations to succeed.

Two of our boys who had decided to join their families in the United States called us one Friday evening from the Consulate. They had missed the last train before the beginning of Shabbat. I told them to catch the next train to Versailles, and announced the arrival to the director of the B Home. Upon their arrival at the station of Versailles, they asked for directions to the castle. They were sent to the Château de Versailles and searched it from top to bottom without finding any children. One of the attendants explained to them how to find the proper, much smaller, castle. When I asked them whether the Château de Versailles had not seemed a bit too magnificent to be a children's home, their innocent answer was, "Not at all!"

Reality was going to be a great shock for them.

Chapter Four

Uncles From America and Elsewhere

Kalman Rosenblum was the first to leave Taverny for the United States. His was a true odyssey. He tracked down two elder brothers who had been living in Cochabamba, Bolivia, since 1939. They had arranged for Kalman's visa and were anxious to see him. We informed the H.I.C.E.M. (a Jewish organization in charge of emigrations), which promised to take care of all the procedures.

Like his comrades, Kalman only believed in what he saw with his own eyes. He made inquiries in Paris and told us that there was no Bolivian consulate in France. Unable to believe this, we called the H.I.C.E.M., who claimed that the boy had misunderstood. They said that there was, of course, a Bolivian consulate in Paris—all one needed was some patience. Kalman showed us guides and telephone books to prove that Bolivia was not listed among the consulates, but the H.I.C.E.M. insisted otherwise.

Another letter arrived from Kalman's brothers. The visa was no longer valid, but they had succeeded in obtaining a six-month extension. They warned Kalman that the trip from Paris to Lisbon, Portugal and the six-week journey by ship had to be included in this time period. We constantly harassed the H.I.C.E.M. and they, in return, repeatedly stated: "We are taking care of everything."

At about the same time, Niny accompanied a little girl of the O.S.E. to London. Coming through West End she noticed the Bolivian Consulate and inquired about their office in Paris. She was told that, indeed, there was none! All consular matters for France and England had to be directed to the London office. The consul agreed to see her and she told him Kalman Rosenblum's story. To her surprise, he opened a drawer, pulled out a visa and said, "I have been waiting for eight months for the owner of this visa. Never before has a six month visa for Bolivia been renewed." Niny stayed in London to wait for Kalman's visa, but the consul could do nothing for her: first the transit visas for Brazil, Portugal, and Spain had to be obtained. Geographically and administratively, the Bolivian visa was last in sequence.

Niny, Kalman and I were pushed from consulate to consulate in the totally disorganized, nerve-racking atmosphere of post-war Paris. Kalman obtained a boat ticket but, for reasons totally unknown to us, was unable to obtain a Spanish visa and we decided that he would take a boat from Bordeaux to Lisbon in order to stay within the time limit. The consul of London told us on the telephone to send him Kalman's passport and promised to send it back personally by return mail. What a relief! Kalman packed his suitcase—but the letter from London never arrived. Each time we called London, we were told that the visa would be sent the following day.

Kalman unpacked and said: "I knew it, I'll never see my brothers." The visa finally arrived on the eve of the boat's departure from Bordeaux. Niny, Kalman and I engaged in a crazy time-race: Taverny to Paris—Niny at the travel agency—Kalman and myself at the Austerlitz station lining up to buy the ticket for Bordeaux. At last, Kalman jumped onto the last car of the train packed with Portuguese and Spanish emigrants, and was surrounded by luggage and children. The engine whistled and the train started off; Niny arrived just in time to hand the ticket to Kalman. He was the first boy to leave us and we did not even have time to say goodbye.

After we had waited three months, a long letter written in Yiddish arrived from Kalman. Moshe read it to us after dinner that evening and everyone listened in total silence. Each of Kalman's friends was a candidate for emigration and was anxious to learn about his ordeals. The letter contained this essential passage:

My two brothers received me very well, but they do not understand me. It is very hot here and everybody wears short sleeves. My brothers show everyone the camp numbers tattooed on my arms. I am an odd creature, a living museum piece. My brothers and I don't speak the same language. I am going to find work, save most of my salary, and then return to Taverny. Write to me quickly to tell me that my place is not taken.

No one was able to speak. Moshe continued reading. There was a post-script:

Niny, I love you. I was afraid to tell you. Please, wait for me. When I come back, we'll get married.

A roar of laughter eased the unbearable tension created by Kalman's letter.

Niny kept a cool head and decided not to answer Kalman's note. "It would be absurd to have him come back," she said. "There is no future for him over here—he has to forget the past and make a new life for himself. Within two years, Taverny will no longer exist for him. He'll be sad for a month or two—then he'll forget." This was our decision: no matter how heartbreaking it would be for them, we would not reply to the boys' distressing letters.

In the beginning, Kalman worked as a delivery man in Cochachamba, practiced all sorts of trades, and finally opened his own business. Within twenty years he became an internationally known businessman in La Paz. During a trip to Paris he went to the O.S.E. and asked for Niny. It took us two weeks to find her but Kalman waited patiently. When he met Niny he said to her, "Have you waited for me? I live in La Paz, but once we are married, we'll move wherever you want." Niny, however, already had a husband and children.

Many other boys were found by uncles, aunts or remote cousins who had left Central Europe before the war and

47

had moved to the United States, South America or Australia. The news about the extermination of Jews by the Nazis had come as a shock to them and they blamed themselves for having lived a carefree life. When they recognized the name of one of their relatives on the lists of survivors, they sought to make amends. Thus, many of our young people received news from an uncle or a remote parent unknown to them in most cases. They wrote in warm terms, invited the youngsters to join them, and sent money for the journey along with an affidavit, an essential document for the emigration visa; a ticket usually followed soon after.

We were convinced that all of these persons were rich and generous "godparents," and that Brooklyn, where most letters came from, was the "Champs Elysées" of New York. We did not know that, in fact, Brooklyn was a poor section of New York, the scenery of *West Side Story,* with crumbling, red brick houses and outside staircases, or that the uncles or cousins were factory workers and even their children had to do hard labor. In many cases, their mothers contributed the money needed for the voyage by cleaning houses.

Even though an American visa was not as difficult to obtain as Kalman's, it was still an extremely complicated procedure. The American Consulate, located in Place de la Concorde at the time, requested not only a passport and a certificate of good character, but a great number of documents about the emigrant. Then, after a certain period of time, the applicant was called for a final interview.

When it was Meyer-Tzvi's turn, I reminded him that he was supposed to be 17 years old, and not 21 as it was much easier to obtain a visa for the underaged. We suggested that he shave his beard to look younger, but Meyer-Tzvi explained that several hundred members of his father's former congregation were waiting for him in New York and had prepared a house for him. He was going to be their community's rabbi and could not very well arrive beardless. Under these circumstances, I let him go to the consulate by himself, even though he understood neither English nor French. On the following day he proudly returned to Taverny

48

with his passport and a visa for the United States.

A few weeks before his departure he showed me a picture of a lovely young girl and told me that she was his fiancée and that he would like us to organize a special dinner party in their honor. I was dumbfounded. Meyer-Tzvi explained to me that the rabbi of a community had to be a married man, and that he had to arrive in New York at least engaged. "I heard about a young girl from my home town, a remote cousin, who had survived and was living in a displaced persons camp," he said. "I wrote to her and we became engaged. As soon as she can come to the United States we shall get married." So, on a Saturday evening after Sabbath, we celebrated this quite unusual engagement with the young girl's photo pinned to the wall. She had to wait two years before getting a visa. They were married immediately upon her arrival and are now a very happy couple.

The most unforeseen complications arose at times, as in the case of the two boys who had used a friend's train season-ticket that was strictly reserved for the owner. They had been caught and a police report had been filed. The boys paid no attention to the incident, but, in the end, had to appear in court. Without a clean police record their departure for the United States was endangered. The only solution was for the director of the French railroad to withdraw the complaint. Since he was an important official, obtaining this withdrawl was not an easy task, but he eventually complied with my request and the boys were able to leave for America.

When Simon was about to embark, he received a letter informing him that his mother was still alive in their home town in Czechoslovakia. He wrote to her and she asked him to come live with her. It was a very delicate situation for Simon. On the one hand, he wanted to leave for the United States, but on the other hand, he wished to see his mother first. Crossing the border with an American visa, however, would jeopardize his return. He decided to see the Czechoslovakian consul in Paris, who persuaded him not to go there. The consul suggested that he meet his mother in the first hotel of Prague where they would not be harassed, and issued Simon a diplomatic passport.

Prague was decorated with flags and banners, and an impressive number of soldiers and policemen surrounded the station. Not realizing what he was doing, Simon asked one of them what the occasion was. He had to show his passport and the policeman exclaimed, "How strange! You carry a diplomatic passport and yet you don't know that Marshal Tito, the leader of Yugoslavia, is coming on an official visit? That is unusual indeed. Take him to the police station."

His young age also made the authorities suspicious about his function as a diplomat. Simon asked them to call the consul. It took several hours to reach him, but in the end the counsul vouched for his employee. Simon was released and raced to the hotel. He and his mother did not leave the premises for three days, not caring about the festivities around them. Simon persuaded his mother to follow him to the United States, and a few years later she rejoined him there. She greatly contributed to her son's strife for an independent life.

As for the Czechoslovakian consul in Paris, he was recalled to his country and disappeared. Neither Simon nor anyone else ever heard of him again.

The Cow and Its Friend

Every one called Herschel Birnbaum "Katsef," the "butcher," for he had learned his father's trade and worked at Olida, a meat factory. Katsef had been lucky to find a truly rich uncle in America who was a powerful businessman, but the butcher had no intentions of changing his way of life. In the evenings he would don a pair of tight, worn-out trousers, a much too small coat, and down-to-the-heel shoes, screw a filthy, shiny cap onto his head, and rush to take care of our cow. We did, indeed, own a cow in Taverny. It had been left behind by the rabbi from Klausenburg who had survived the camp and was on his way to the United States. He had liked everything about our home, except that there was no Kosher milk. Kosher milk is nothing other than regular cowmilk, drawn under the surveillance of a Jew to avoid the addition of donkey milk. (Donkey meat and milk are forbidden under Jewish law.)

We had put the cow up in the former stables and our country boys were delighted, fighting for the right to draw the milk and to curry her during the first few days. Then the butcher took over; he called the cow Judith and truly loved her. Katsef, however, had committed a great sin—he had eaten pork sausage at the meat factory and went to atone at the nearby yeshiva in Fublaines. He asked me to take care of Judith during his two-week absence: "It is winter now and the cow cannot go outside, but she needs exercise. Please have her run around the park three times each day."

I, of course, quickly forgot about his instructions. One evening, returning late from Paris, I heard the heartbreaking moans and lowings of the cow. I rushed to the telephone to call the vet while our janitor led the cow out of the stables. She slumped to the ground, never getting up again and the vet could do nothing but witness her death. The cow's belly had swollen terribly and the doctor told me: "The cow lacked exercise; it should have been taken out. The hay was also too wet." What would I say to the butcher?

The boys watched silently as we spread a blanket over the cow. After their departure for work on the following day, I took the necessary measures to have the animal removed. While I was waiting for the truck to arrive, I heard terrible moaning once again. Crouching next to the cow was the butcher, crying his heart out. "Last night I dreamt the cow had died," he said. "I jumped onto the first train to make sure that it had only been a dream. But it wasn't a dream. . . ."

These events finally prompted the butcher to take up his uncle's invitation to go to Cincinnati. Because he had sent him a first-class plane ticket that only rich people could afford at that time, Niny and I decided to buy Herschel proper clothing and a suitcase so that he would not feel awkward on the plane. We stood waiting for him at the Orly terminal in Paris, a very luxurious airport where diplomats and their elegant wives strolled up and down the aisles, followed by porters carrying their trunks and leather travel bags. We had been well advised to buy a decent outfit for Herschel! But when he arrived, Herschel was empty-handed and dressed in his everyday clothes. Seeing the dismay on our faces, he explained that his uncle in Cincinnati was definitely rich enough to buy him new clothes and that there was no reason for him to travel in new garments. He had distributed all of his possessions, including the items we had purchased for him, to those who had nothing. The stewardess was unable to believe that he travelled without any luggage; his fellow passengers looked at him in disgust. Herschel was the true, lonely, wandering Jew who left nothing behind and did not know what the future would bring.

Like so many others, he wrote to us: "My uncle does not understand me. I am going to leave him." He settled in New York where he became a furrier, and enjoyed an excellent reputation. He married a young, non-Jewish American woman and apparently never talked about his youth to his two sons. Then, one day, he jumped out of a window and killed himself.

Eric—The Last Ones Will be First

One after the other, about forty of our children left for the United States. The house emptied, and the O.S.E. asked us to take children in transit, or temporary guests with special problems.

The first one to arrive was Eric, a child who had been born without hands or feet. He was 16, but looked about six. His father, a doctor in Vienna, had applied for visas to America for his entire family when Austria was annexed to Germany in 1938. He only received three: for his wife, his daughter—a beautiful girl eight years older than Eric—and for himself. Only people in good health were accepted by America, and Eric was refused entry. The parents were about to cancel their departure, but the consul was adamant: "Leave, you have no choice. In five years you will be American citizens and you will be able to have your son join you."

52

Unhappy and broken-hearted, Eric's parents left their son with his grandmother in Antwerp. On May 10, 1940, the Germans entered neutral Belgium and chaos broke out. The exodus to southern France followed. The grandmother left with her grandson and died on the road during a bombardment in Rouen. The little boy was brought to an orphanage and stayed there until the end of the war. As early as 1945, his parents started procedures to find him and were greatly helped in their search by the child's physical handicap. They found him, paid the pension for the years he spent in the orphanage, and asked the O.S.E. to keep Eric in a children's home until they could obtain a visa for him.

The O.S.E. was convinced that our boys, who had seen just about everything, would have no problems accepting Eric. But for me, it was a shock. Upon my return from a trip to Paris, I saw a little five or six-year-old boy perched on a chair, knitting a long, red scarf. The knitting needles seemed to move by themselves, firmly tucked into the sleeves of his coat. Large tears ran down his cheeks to his harelip. I had to step out of my office to regain my senses. When I re-entered, he explained with his thin, little voice that he had been waiting for a long time but was afraid to leave the office on his own. I took him to the dining room and the other boys accepted him quite simply and naturally. He had been very afraid of this moment—of meeting strange people, of scaring them—but everything had gone well.

Eric ate very properly, tucking fork, spoon or knife into his sleeve. He would have been lost with short sleeves. He moved very quickly on his stumps and soon became everyone's friend, teaching the boys French and writing letters for them. He abhorred being treated like a child—after all, he was 16 years old.

During a trip to the American consulate in Paris an unfortunate incident occurred on the train. The ticket controller and passengers felt great pity for the child and asked, "What happened to your little boy? Was it an accident or was he born like that?" It was an excruciating train ride for all of us.

Eric was terrified of strangers and hid in his room when guests arrived for Sabbath. We respected his fear and brought dinner to his room. After the visitors left, he would come downstairs, smiling and relieved.

Having graduated from school, Eric refused to continue his studies, but I insisted he do so for I was convinced that keeping busy was as good for him as for everyone else. I drove him to school on the handle-bar of my bicycle and when I picked him up after his first day, he was beaming with joy. No one had asked any questions. He made friends with a black boy, who was as different from the others as himself, and became the best student of his class.

His parents and married sister wrote to him regularly. One day they sent a package containing clothing for a young 16-year-old boy. We sent a photo of Eric to his parents, and had to use all our tact and skill to break the news of Eric's condition to them.

When Eric was ready to embark for the United States, I put him in the custody of a tall, strong boy who was also going there. The letter we received from the tall boy convinced us once more that those who are last, often come first in the end:

> *It was a horrible trip. We travelled on the Liberty Ship (an American transport that had carried troops and material to France at the time of the invasion and had been converted to a passenger ship later on). I was sick throughout the voyage and could not leave my cabin. I was very fortunate to have Eric, who took care of me without tiring; he was constantly on the go.*

We were without any news from Eric for a long time. A letter finally arrived: "I wasn't able to write to you sooner because my parents put me into a hospital as soon as I arrived. The doctors made me wear prostheses on my arms and legs. I am very unhappy for I cannot manage with them. I have lost my freedom of movement. I am writing to you in the middle of the night and have secretly removed the devices. I would like to come back. . . ."

Despite his unfortunate travel at sea, Eric's companion

joined the American Navy and signed up for 25 years. He is now a brilliant, high-ranking officer and spends only short periods of time on land to see his wife and children in New York.

France and Francois

After Eric's departure, the O.S.E. sent us a rabbi and his large family who were waiting to embark for the United States. In order to escape the Germans, the rabbi had been living in a forest during the war, moving from hiding place to hiding place with his wife and their ten children. In addition to his own family, the rabbi's sister had given him the charge of her two boys. He thus had twelve children, aged five to 21. Unable to trace the nephews' parents after the war, the rabbi married them to his oldest daughters.

The rabbi was a very gentle and well-bred man, who left the responsibility of their children to his extremely active wife. I started to become impatient, although polite, about their prolonged sojourn in our house, especially because the oldest daughter was about to give birth. Eventually, they moved to Paris. Several days after their departure the newspapers brought the story of a couple that had embarked as blind passengers on the *France* in Le Havre. The man had been discovered and was forced to leave the ship, but the woman could not be found. During the night, wailings coming from a covered lifeboat led to the discovery of a young woman who did not speak any French and was about to give birth. A little girl was born in the infirmary and was baptized "France."

I was overcome by a wave of remorse at the idea of the shy, young woman giving birth on a ship among strangers, and I decided to visit her family at their Paris hotel. When I questioned her husband as to whether he had been at Le Havre, he replied, "Yes. My wife is still there; they are unable to find her!" I congratulated him: "Mazel Tov! You have a daughter!" I gave him the translation of the article about the circumstances of France's birth and the father exclaimed furiously, "How dare they give her a name! She'll be called Sara-Rivka, just as we had decided!" Being born on a French vessel, the little girl was issued a French passport and the nursing mother was permitted to accompany her. That is how a new-born child enabled its parents to settle in the United States—the father had no problems obtaining an American passport.

Our last guest was a 17-year-old boy named Francois. He had lost all of his family in deportation and had been to every single children's home of the O.S.E., each of them having expelled him. To my great surprise, though, I found him to be a calm, extremely gentle young man with excellent manners. He spoke French very well and I had him take over the office, answering the telephone, doing the correspondence, and running errands. He efficiently took over part of my manifold activities. I also gave him the cash box containing the boys' pocket money and put him in charge of distributing it. He administered our monthly budget as well.

After his departure for the United States, the O.S.E. called to find out how I had managed to keep Francois, an "inveterate cleptomaniac," for such a long time. At first, I was quite furious at the idea that they had dared to send a cleptomaniac to a children's home without informing us, but then again, had I been warned in advance, I probably would not have entrusted Francois with the pocket money and the budget. Confidence had proven to be the best therapy.

The boys who had not been able to find their parents returned to their initial dream—to go to Palestine. The British government, however, had stopped all permits to enter. Palestine had become a tightly secured fortress where Jews were not admitted.

Weary of waiting in the German camps for a hypothetical international solution, many displaced Jews attempted to force the British blockade by entering Palestine illegally. Travelling under inconceivable circumstances, sailing in old, worn-out crafts, they endangered their lives time and again. In most cases they reached the promised land at night. To counter these illegal efforts, the British government confined the immigrants to camps on Cyprus. Thus, many thousands of Jews were once again fenced in behind barbed wire.

Fully aware of the dangers of embarking for Palestine, the young people of Taverny were hesitant to leave. A dozen of them decided to take the risk and started off, either alone or in groups. All of them succeeded except for one, who was taken to Cyprus.

We all know that a large ship, the Exodus, was chartered for thousands of displaced persons. At its arrival in Haifa, the British authorities refused entry to the port and the ship returned to Port-Vendres, and from there went to Hamburg. Eleven of our children were on board the Exodus. Some found the courage to try the odyssey again—others returned to France and settled in Paris.

The last child to remain in Taverny had discovered relatives in Australia, but was reluctant to leave: "I have never had a family life; I don't know what it is like. I'm much too afraid of being engulfed by it now."

By the end of 1947 everyone had left Taverny and the Castle of Vaucelles was closed down. Niny settled in Paris and I went to Strasburg. Both of us went on to raise families. Neither of us ever talked about the past. The ties had been severed; why revive the memories? We were convinced that we would never see or hear about the children of Ambloy and Taverny again.

Chapter Five

Twenty Years Later: New York

In the Spring of 1965, Niny and I received invitations to a dinner being held in New York to commemorate the 20th anniversary of the liberation of Buchenwald. The invitation was signed: "Committee of the Buchenwald-Taverny Group."

A cable followed: "Come. You are our guest. Cable date of your arrival." Niny was unable to attend, so I travelled alone. During the flight I closely studied a large photo of the Ambloy group. Twenty years had passed and I feared that I would not recognize them.

They stood waiting behind the large glass front at Kennedy Airport, holding bouquets of flowers and the same photo of Ambloy. They, too, mistrusted their memories. A wave of emotion swept over us as we greeted each other. It was obvious that the many years of silence had not severed the bonds of affection between us.

The Dinner—We are the Dead Resurrected by God

Most of the former inmates arrived during the evening from different parts of the United States. Many of them had not seen each other since Taverny. They used their former nicknames such as "redhead," but the redhead had since gone bald. Unable to perceive the reasons for our emotion, the wives remained reserved.

Among the members of the "Committee" presiding over the dinner party were Mr. Margulies and Moshe, tall and

59

respectable with a long grey beard. Moshe rose and started with the blessing: "Blessed be Thou, King of the World, who allowed us to live and to attain this day." The attendants rose to their feet and ardently repeated the words. He then continued: "We have not gathered today to glory in being alive, but to remember those who are dead. Tonight's gathering is meant as a continuation of the Yom Kippur in Ambloy when some had refused to say Yzkor. Today, we know that our parents and our relatives will never return. We have been struggling for twenty years to succeed in our new lives. They have been difficult years during which we had neither the time nor the peace of mind to mourn our parents, our brothers and sisters, our families and our villages. The time has come now when we can do so. Let us rise and think of them, let us say Kadish—the prayer for the dead." Everyone cried and recited Kadish aloud, together.

After a long moment of silence, Moshe continued in his strong voice: "We are the remains of Ezekiel having recovered our breath. We are the dead God has resurrected. Let us celebrate. For Passover, we have unleavened bread, for Hannukkah[1] the candles, for the Feast of Tabernacles[2] the shed ... And here is what I have found for our celebration." He held up a cracked bowl filled with potatoes. "None of you have forgotten how much potatoes meant to us in Buchenwald, be they raw or cooked, peeled or not. Just the peelings were treasured possessions!" He continued his speech, mixing laughter with tears and despair with hope. He was their good old Moshe of twenty years ago.

The dinner progressed with an affectionate, warm and fervent atmosphere. Mr. Margulies spoke of the common past that had tied a strong bond between the survivors of Buchenwald. He said how happy he was that so many had come. The aim of Taverny, to create a home and a substitute family, had been fulfilled; the ties of affection had remained strong and lasting.

I was then asked to make a speech.

[1] Holiday commemorating the rededication of the Temple of Jerusalem after the victory of Judas Maccabeus over the Greek in 165 B.C.
[2] Celebrated in Autumn during seven days.

60

I transmitted regards from Niny and explained the reasons for our silence—for not replying to their letters in the beginning. I told them that whenever Niny and I met, we spoke of them with great warmth. I then addressed the wives, who must have felt overlooked to a certain degree: "Thanks to you, your husbands are happy and content. You are the ones who helped them find peace and happiness." They were deeply touched by these words.

During the dinner, they gave me a bracelet inscribed with the words: "To Judith—For the twentieth anniversary—The boys of Buchenwald and Taverny." But I had received much more than their gift. They all had wanted to see me, to present their families to me, and they had started talking about their pasts—many of them for the first time in their lives. In Taverny, we had never asked any questions, the subject being much too painful at the time. But twenty years later in New York, I felt the desire to find out about their mothers and families, about the kind of education they had received. Had the camps influenced their behavior, the choices they had made? How did they raise their children? How did they view their lives? Some of their responses were short and incomplete, while others were lengthy. Names have been changed, but all accounts were rendered spontaneously, and I have written them down exactly as they were told.

The children of Buchenwald who met in the United States seemed to have found a sense of security by integrating into American life, while preserving the Jewish tradition within their families and communities.

Their refusal to speak about the camps to relatives, and even more so to strangers, was dictated by a sense of self-preservation—they wanted to forget. They had been so deeply humiliated that they shied away from arousing the pity of others; this would have been just another type of humiliation. In their struggle for success they sought to atone for having remained alive.

They kept their nightmares to themselves for they knew that only those who had lived through the same ordeals could understand, and each of them had endured the camps in a different way.

My former boys of Taverny refused to take me to a new bar on the 66th floor of a sky-scraper. The number of their barracks, 66, will remain in their minds forever as the memory of indescribable sufferings.

David—Wealth and Remorse

David is the boy who had brought a violin from Weimar. At his arrival in Ambloy, he was 19 years old and had decided to become a dental technician. He is now living with his wife and three children in a large house in a wealthy suburb of New York. In this home he told his story, but only to me:

> *I was born in Czechoslovakia in 1929. There were six children in our family, three girls and three boys. Shortly before the war, my father had sent my older sister to New York. I was first deported to Auschwitz with my older brother Abraham, then to other camps, where I frequently met my cousin Moshe, the rabbi. The three of us were together in Buchenwald when it was liberated. When the SS ordered us to leave the camp, Moshe advised us to disobey. If we had stepped through the gate, kicked out by the Germans, we would have been shot. At the gate, I decided to play dead and let myself fall near the dead bodies lying on the side of the road. An SS soldier struck me hard on the head but, despite the pain, I did not move. A terrible confusion mingled with blows and screams surrounding me and then, suddenly, there was dead silence. I waited about 30 minutes before I opened my eyes and lifted my head; I saw a huge tank and black American soldiers who were chewing gum. I thought: "This must be the secret weapon of the Americans, some super-intelligent ruminating animal!" I then fainted.*
>
> *Later, I contracted typhus and a Czechoslovakian doctor saved my life. When I was allowed to leave the infirmary, Moshe stole chickens because our mothers had always pretended that chicken soup was a cure for*

62

everything. I gave my sister's address in the United States to an American soldier and asked him to inform her that Abraham and I were alive. He delivered the message.

Fifteen years later, a man stepped into my New York office. He was that soldier, and we recognized each other immediately.

We departed for France after leaving Buchenwald. My uncle had sent visas and affidavits and we embarked for New York.

When I asked David what he remembered about the children's homes he had been in, he told me the following:

I have only vague memories of Ambloy and Taverny. The same goes for the camps—I have completely forgotten the details. We were handed everything at Taverny; all complications were kept from us. We thought that everything was our due because we had survived. In a way, we lived outside of reality. When we arrived in the United States, we thought we would be entering a paradise with angels there to hold our hands. We had to learn about the facts of life the hard way and we should have been prepared for it. I suffered a terrible depression during the first week. My uncle knew what had happened in the camps. As for me, I had been quick to realize that talking about the past would make me an outsider. The people here thought: "It is over. Forget about the past and show us what you can do." My uncle, his wife, Abraham, and myself set off to find work in all kinds of factories. I didn't understand a word of English and all day I saw people shaking their heads in refusal. I felt like an unwanted calf being led to market.

One evening, while walking home to my older sister's apartment where I lived with Abraham, I came to a factory that made electric watches for sports events. One thing led to another and I was hired to guard the building during the absences of the owner, who later taught me how to perforate and cut pieces of metal according to a pattern. That was my first job. Several others followed until I started working on my own. Eventually, I acquired

63

several drugstores and became engaged in real estate.

I had enormous problems adjusting to the American way of life. American culture, based on material values only, seemed extremely shallow. After two years of living in the United States, I still did not speak English. I had been torn from affectionate surroundings where I had felt at home and was projected into a society where I was nothing. I was 21 years old, but unable to speak, to understand, to function. I took evening courses and was conferred a high school diploma. By 1949 I didn't feel as lost anymore—I could at least speak and understand the language—and I started going places with my cousin, Fanny, who was born in this country. She helped me to understand the United States.

My manner was greatly influenced by my past. I had been deported at age 18 and had no idea what it meant to fight back while risking your own life. When I saw the movie Holocaust *on television, I felt very ashamed of myself and of those seemingly intelligent and deter- mined persons who did not realize that one had to show physical courage to survive and had to stake his own life to resist the enemy. Ignorant of this fact, I and thousands of others had been trapped like a herd of sheep, unable to show the slightest resistance. By rebelling against our rabbis, the insurgents of Warsaw have, by far, exceeded their own courage. God works miracles only if we, our- selves, contribute. I am ashamed of the doctrines of our religion that emphasize passivity and regard suffering as a punishment of God.*

Since I was the first-born, my father sent me to a yeshiva and I was very pious at my arrival in the United States. But I have gradually relinquished all command- ments and have ceased living by them altogether.

When my children were very young, I went to see my cousin Moshe to tell him that I did not intend to raise them as my father had raised me. I had been compelled to be the most knowledgeable, the most pious of all. Moshe said to me: "You are going to regret it," and he was right. Although I wanted to raise my children under the Jewish tradition, I decided to free them from the obligation to excel. Today, I know that my attitude has kept them from fully developing their capacities: my children lack ambition. I should have made them realize that they have a mission to accomplish. Had I the opportunity, I would have led a very religious Jewish life in a Zionist section of Jerusalem.

I asked David how he felt about the Germans.

Asking for compensation from the Germans has been a great ordeal. Nothing can ever be done to redeem the terrible sufferings in the camps. To this day I curse the Germans and say: "Let them all die!" Yet, I do not hate everything about the Germans—I just hate their philosophy. Hitler was not a misconception of nature. He was the product of the philosophy of Nietzsche, Kant and Hegel, glorifying the superman, the superior creature. Hitler was nothing but an instrument accomplishing the conviction of German mentality that feeble and unproductive persons ought to be killed.

During a group trip through Europe a few years ago, I had to pass through Germany. I was amazed. In my mind, all Germans looked like the SS soldiers in the camps: tall, erect, dressed in black—true supermen. I was astonished by the two customs officers that checked our passports at the border. One of them was short and fat, the other was carrying a small purse. I asked myself, "Are these the supermen who overawed us in the camps?" I was furious to realize that they had been strong enough to impose their superiority on me. I was humiliated by what they had done to my mind.

During my two-day stay in Germany I closely watched each man, thinking: "Could this one have been a guard?" They, however, sang and drank beer and were totally oblivious and without remorse. . . .

To think that some historians dare proclaim that the camps never existed. . . !

Although he became an American businessman by his own means, David, like many others, was deeply marked by his life in the camps. He has severed all ties to his past and to the moral values which had governed his childhood, for they had not generated the strength in him to resist the strains of concentration camp life. He has also become fascinated by the overwhelming power of his torturers. As a defense mechanism, he identifies with his aggressors. Anna Freud explained this phenomenon in 1936: "When faced with outside danger, the victim identifies himself with his aggressor, either by imitating his physical and moral attitudes, or by adopting some of the specific power symbols for himself."[1]

David strived to reach this power by choosing material values. The lure of money was an illusion though, as it left him alone without friends or ideals. He appears to have suffered "survivor syndrome." Individuals with this syndrome feel a "heavy burden coupled with a sense of guilt for having survived, forcing him into isolation and beyond the limits of his social surroundings."[2]

I met David again in 1980. He had sold his drugstores and retired to Florida with his wife. Their three children had left home and David did not want to talk about it. What had happened? We do not know for sure, but it seems that his children, the second generation, were deeply affected by their father's distress. They had become indirect victims of Nazi persecutions.

Moshe: The "Responsa"

First in the camp, and later in Taverny, Moshe had been a "leader." Today, Moshe has become an orthodox rabbi who closely abides by the written text yet is open to modern technology. He is famous throughout the Jewish world for his books of "responsa" which offer the religious Jew solu-

[1]Freud A. The Ego and the Mechanisms of Defense, New York, Inter. Univ. Press, 1964, page 72.
[2]Krystal H. and Niederland W.G. Clinical Observation of the Survivor Syndrome ed. Massive Psychic Trauma, New York, Inter. Univ. Press, 1966, page 344.

tions to problems created by modern life. He gave me the following account of his past:

I was born in Czechoslovakia in 1925. My father was head of a yeshiva and a collel, a yeshiva for adults. Of the six children in our family, I was the fifth. I went to a Czechoslovakian school for two years and then to heder and the yeshiva. My father had links with the outside world and realized what was going to happen. He succeeded in getting me a visa for the Holy Land in 1942, but it was already too late. When we were deported in 1944, my father had no illusions. Convinced that he was going to die, he used the water distributed by the Germans to wash his hands and recited the prayer for the dead.

I was completely alone when I came to Auschwitz. I refuse to talk about this period; I never mention it to my children. But the nightmares return every night.

Thanks to an affidavit granted by an uncle in New York, I was able to leave for the United States in 1947. After two days, however, feeling very unhappy, I left my uncle who was not a religious man. I searched for the address of the rabbi of Klausenburg who had visited us in Taverny and was very well received by him. Eighteen months later I was head of one of his yeshivoth and soon after I opened my own school. In the beginning it was small and poor but it now occupies several buildings. I have a tremendous influence on my pupils. After getting married, they settle in this neighborhood and become members of my congregation. I have opened a kindergarten and intend to set up a heder and a school.

The upsurge of religious life in the United States is largely due to the concentration camps. Before the war there were 800 pupils in the yeshivoth, now there are 50,000. I am very proud to have participated in this development. My own children are raised in the spirit of my father's convictions. But I am even more strict with them than he was with me: I never make any concessions.

67

Deportation has taught me that you can only rely on yourself and never on a non-Jew. I believe that in writing this book you have undertaken a very important task. Auschwitz must never be forgotten.

Moshe has remained close friends with Isaie, a Polish boy who had gone from Taverny to Jerusalem to live with his rabbi from Gour. To accept a Hungarian Jew into the Hassidic world of a Polish rabbi would have been unthinkable before the war.

Isaie had shown Moshe's books of responsa to the rabbi from Gour. Extremely impressed by the books and the author, he then proposed a marriage between his nephew and Moshe's oldest daughter with hopes of creating a dynasty. The two young people met, liked each other, and were later married. This union has a symbolic meaning for the rabbi of Gour: a reconciliation with Hungarian Judaism. Isaie and Moshe were convinced that it was a direct result of Taverny.

At one time, large posters sent from New York covered the walls of the houses in Jerusalem. Moshe was going to lay the corner stone for a new religious quarter in the north of that city. All Hassidic rabbis of note had come. Moshe, in his speech, evoked his home town and the Jews who had lived there. Most of them had been exterminated and his aim was to bring this community back to life in the Holy Land, the cradle of religious life, where the yearning of the Jewish people had begun.

At the end of his speech, Moshe turned to me and said, "I hope I did not disappoint you." I was deeply moved.

Raphael and Friendship

Raphael was the little boy who, in his despair, left his room at Taverny only at nighttime to smell the wind. In New York I learned about the wonderful memories he has kept of his childhood in Rumania. He talked about his sweet and affectionate mother and about Auschwitz:

At the time of my arrival in Auschwitz I was only 15

years old but already very tall. On the first day, the Germans heaved a rail onto the shoulders of six men, the two tallest at each end of the rail. The smallest, in the middle, lifted their shoulders a little, pretending to help, but the heavy load remained on the two tall ones. I was placed in the front at first, and when we returned I was put in the back, but the weight was still the same. All I saw was my comrades' backs. The weight of the rail and the terrible effort it took to carry it were enough to make me cry. That evening in the barracks, I saw that the other tall boy was crying, too. It was Moshe, and from that day on we remained together, sharing everything. He saved my life twice. The first time was in Buchenwald a few days before the arrival of the Americans. A Ukranian soldier had hit me hard on the head, almost paralyzing me, and I remained sprawled on my cot for several days until hunger drove me out. An SS soldier yelled at me: "What are you doing here?" Moshe just happened to come by. Any other prisoner would have continued on his way, but Moshe stopped and spoke to the SS soldier: "Leave him alone. I know him. He's not normal, he's crazy." The SS turned away and I was able to return to the barracks.

The second time was after liberation. I had overeaten and was deathly sick with diarrhea. Moshe nursed me tirelessly for three weeks. He burnt bread and gave it to me as a kind of coal. I would have died without him. I know that he doesn't need me now, but I feel that I am not grateful enough and would like to be able to do something for him. I also contracted typhus in Buchenwald. It was Moshe again who put my name on the list of people leaving for France. When it was time to leave, he picked me up at the hospital and carried me in his arms to the train. Once, during our stay in Ecouis, we were taken on a sightseeing tour of Paris and visited the Eiffel Tower. The elevator was out of order and Myer-Tzvi, having had his feet frozen once, could barely walk. I remembered what Moshe had done for me and I carried Myer-Tzvi in my arms. But by the time we had reached the first level, the other boys were already on their way back down, so I quietly turned around to follow them for fear of getting lost.

In Taverny, I learned my father's trade—printing. I traced my elder sister, who was living in Sweden, but I was unable to obtain a visa to join her there. I tried to go to Israel on the Exodus: eleven places were available, and I was the twelfth. When Taverny was closed down, two other boys and I went to a yeshiva near Paris. The members of this school were preparing to leave for the United States, and after their departure the three of us had nowhere to go. We soon found another group, the "Wise men of Lublin," who obtained visas for the United States for us. But their yeshiva in New York did not accept me because I did not have the money to pay for room and board. Once more, I had nowhere to go. Finally, Meyer-Tzvi put me up in the large house where an unmarried uncle of his lived. I was given the opportunity to study at the yeshiva run by the rabbi of Klausenburg.

I felt terribly lonely until I met Tibor and Yossi, my comrades from Taverny. Every morning I used to pray in a little synagogue near Myer-Tzvi's house, but one day a man noticed me there and expressed the wish to have me as a son-in-law. I was only 19 years old and had no desire to marry. I changed synagogues until I heard that the young girl had wed, but the man was persistent and proposed that I marry his niece, Myriam. One morning, Myer-Tzvi's uncle said, "A young girl has come to see us and I want you to meet her." My friends insisted that I had nothing to lose by meeting this girl and I complied with the uncle's wish. I chatted with Myriam until two o'clock in the morning, and a month later we were engaged. I did not, however, want to get married without having a job. It took me a year to find one. In the meantime, Myriam's uncled taught me how to engrave tombstones for his shop, but I received no pay for six months. I was lucky to be able to live with Myer-Tzvi's uncle for free. I finally started making $20 a week,

70

and after my marriage, was paid an honest, weekly wage of $30. The other boys who had been at Taverny— all 40 of them—came to my wedding.

We have a girl and three boys and I am a very strict father. I want them to be pious but insist that they all learn a trade. I despise abusive language, be it in English or in Yiddish.

I never talk about the camps—my wife can't under- stand why, but my youngest son does. He was once hit by a car and had to remain in the hospital for a long time. He told me that his pain had been such that he could not talk about it.

Raphael told me that he felt at home in Brooklyn, and that he respected the United States because the interests of the Americans were the same as his own. His wife and friends have helped him become independent. Being an American, Myriam gives him security without pushing him to follow the American way of life; its competitive society places far too many demands on him. His wife understands how vital his ties with the past are to him and keeps an open house for his comrades. The only time Raphael left Brooklyn was to travel to Switzerland for his sister's wedding.

Myer-Tzvi—"Because of Our Sins"

We celebrated Myer-Tzvi's engagement to an unknown cousin before he left Taverny for New York. He was not yet twenty, and a New York community awaited his arrival. Being a rabbi and son of a rabbi, he was expected to be married, or at least engaged.

A slim and pleasant woman opened the door to their Brooklyn apartment. The rabbi Myer-Tzvi was seated at a long table covered with white linen. He was an impressive figure with a long beard and heavy glasses, clad in the tra- ditional outfit: pumps, stockings and black pants, a long caftan and a round broad-rimmed hat. I listened to Meyer- Tzvi's account while consuming the cakes and tea that his wife had prepared:

I was born in Hungary in 1925, the eldest of seven children. My father was a well-known rabbi. For two years I lived in a ghetto where I worked very hard. My mother and the six younger children were deported long before I was. I was over 18 years old when my father and I were taken to Auschwitz. The convoy transported 3,500 women and men; 350 were declared fit for work, fit for survival in some way. When we arrived in Buchenwald my father was 40 years old and sensed that we would soon be separated for good. He told me: "Do not change your way of dressing." Pumps and black socks during the week, white socks during Shabbat. I have interpreted this symbolic legacy to mean: respect every single detail of our way of life. Other inmates of Auschwitz interrogated newly-arrived prisoners about what they intended to eat since nothing was kosher. Some answered, "I'll only eat soup." Others said, "I'll eat everything." I told them that I would decide daily. A long-time inmate commented: "You'll see that this one will only eat bread," and he was right. By the time I arrived at Buchenwald, I was totally famished and my toes were frozen. At liberation, I persisted in eating bread only, thus escaping death caused by overeating. I registered to go to France for I was afraid to return to Hungary because of the Russians. I fought a hard battle to obtain kosher food in Ecouis, which brought us to Ambloy, where Moshe and I led a Jewish life.

I was convinced that my younger brother would survive as he was a Talmudic genius and a very tall and strong boy. Yet, he died two weeks before liberation. I had no one left in the world except for three relatives in America—an uncle, an aunt, and a cousin, who I later married. The other members of my family never returned from the camps. My unmarried uncle received me in his house and we still live there. I never went anywhere else.

I am very happy in Brooklyn. Jewish life here completely satisfies me. My children were named after my dead parents, brothers and sisters. Because they were born in this country, they consider themselves Americans

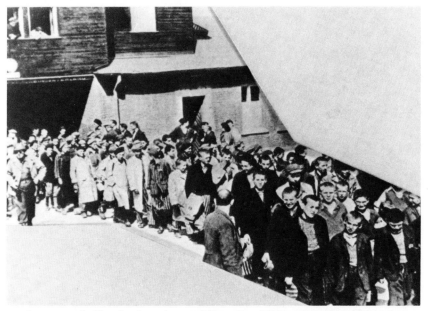

Accompanied by the American soldiers, the children were freed from the gates of Buchenwald and were directed toward the train.

The adolescents' eyes showed sadness and suspicion.

The train carrying the survivors, who were dressed in German uniforms, caused such confusion when it arrived in France, that the words "K.L. (concentration camp) Buchenwald—Orphans" had to be painted on the cars.

Thirty-six years later, at the Convention of Former Concentration Camp Prisoners, held in Jeruslaem in 1981, the children of barracks 66 searched for one another.

The most studious—in the middle—Elie Wiesel.

The improvised synagogue of
Taverny was the center of life.

Judith with some of the
Taverny boys.

The castle of Vaucelles, at Taverny.

Two of the O.S.E. doctors, J. Well and G. Revel, escort the convoy.

An atrocious irony: When the American troops liberated Buchenwald, the only clothing they could find for the children were the uniforms of the Hitler youth.

Niny (standing) surrounded by most of the youngsters.

More identification: a number.

even though only my daughters speak English. I taught my sons the Talmud and mathematics. I want them to have the same Jewish education that I received.

After my arrival in New York, I continued studying the Talmud, mathematics and astronomy on my own. I computed the beginning and end of Shabbat in other towns when members of my congregation went on a trip. Very complicated calculations are required; they have become routine work for me now, but it is a very harassing job.

I am my father's heir. I am in charge of a large community with members who pray in my synagogue and are my students. Because I am extremely well-known, I cannot leave the house and feel very isolated as a result. It is always a great pleasure when the former boys of Taverny come to see me. I never talk about the past to my children; they are not interested. I have, however, written down my memories twice: first by hand and then on the typewriter in 1964. I would not go through the same ordeal again. I wrote the account of our deportation for my children. It occurred after Passover in 1944, an ill-fated period for the Jewish people who had to endure great pains and misfortunes. I was a witness of the terrible calamity that engulfed one third of them, yet I refuse to judge God's will. The Jewish people have been punished for their sins. Their biggest crime had been to believe that they were the chosen people: the Holocaust was God's punishment. I went to great pains to explain some of my sufferings in order to make my children understand that sinners have to accept the wrath of God. They had to be convinced that the Holy law and the strict observance of its commandments were the only way to bring about redemption. We must learn a lesson from the persecutions and sufferings endured in the camps. We must pray even more and never forget our traditions. I am very strict with my children. I want all of them to marry someone who has the same convictions and I want them to dedicate their lives to the Talmud.

73

I returned to New York in 1980. All of Myer-Tzvi's children had married according to their father's wish and had studied in the collel. He has set into practice what his father had demanded in Auschwitz: "Do not change anything," thus conveying a significance to his survival.

Chapter Six

One Day at a Time

Only Plan For the Future

Simon had no qualms about telling his story. The lesson he learned from his past experiences can be summed up as follows: "If you are determined to survive, you will!" As a consequence, he often renders offhand judgments of his comrades. More often than not, though, he lacks consistency. His son wanted to participate in our conversation. In an attempt to visualize what his father had been through, he had visited Dachau on his own. Simon's narrative revealed the truth to him:

I was born in Czechoslovakia in 1927. For us, war began with the German invasion in 1939. Things changed at school—a different mentality took over. I was the third of four children. We spoke several languages— Hungarian, Czechoslovakian, and Russian. My father was very well off. He owned a grocery store and a carrier business that had six or seven horse carriages.

My father was a very pious man although he wore a short beard. He was a Hassid of a rather non-sectarian rabbi. I went to public school to learn languages in the mornings and to heder in the afternoons. Our father conveyed to us the love of work; to him it was a sacred matter. During summer vacations we had to work in the fields.

Once, when I was thirteen, my father fell sick. My

brother was away in the army so I had to take over the distribution of the daily chores to the wagoners. At their return from work in the evening, I invited the wagoners to a nearby bar for a glass of beer. Even before I returned home, my mother found out that I had associated with non-Jews and heavily reprimanded me. I asked her, "What is wrong with inviting your own workmen for a drink? They might have scoffed at my young age, they could have taken advantage of the situation and cheated us. Instead, they did an honest job and deserved being rewarded for it." I had trusted my own judgement and everything had gone well. This is what saved my life in the camps. Those who didn't survive did not die of hunger but died because they thought they would not make it. My older brother was like that. He had given up all hope and I kept telling him, "Be patient, sooner or later it will be over. Struggle each day at a time!" During the long march after the evacuation of Auschwitz the Germans shouted: "Those too tired to continue, get on the trucks!" Before I could hold him back, my brother had followed their order. I never saw him again. This happened on January 22, 1945.

Yes, in the camps one had to be determined to survive, could not believe in miracles, had to be constantly watchful and alert, and needed to work hard. For a while, I was in a small camp near Auschwitz and worked in a metal factory. The head of our barracks remained behind to clean up the quarters and the only tool available to him was a broom. I devised a metal shovel for him at the factory and he was so grateful that he frequently slipped me extra food.

Upon my arrival in Buchenwald, I was taken to the infirmary to be treated for a frozen toe. When I started feeling better, I asked whether I could be of any help. They allowed me to stay even after I was cured and this kept me from starving to death during the days before liberation. When the infirmary was vacated I went to barracks 66. I almost died of overeating after liberation, though, and was deathly sick one week. The idea of

*returning home never struck me. Even the Russians
were reluctant to return to their country. . . . My motto
is: "Never go back. Make a new start and keep looking
ahead!" I was very happy in France. We were treated
like the French prisoners released from German prison
camps. We were handed the same repatriation cards,
had the same advantages as them in the metro and the
trains, and received the same clothing.*

*The Czechoslovakian consul who came to Ecouis was
looking for boys to help him and I volunteered. He called
me to Paris and later sent me to the Hotel de la Reine
d'Angleterre in Biarritz where the families of embassy
employees were living. I remained there for two weeks. I
had no Jewish friends there, though, and wanted to return
to be with my comrades. Thus, I came to Ecouis and
then to Ambloy. I started writing down my memories in
Yiddish, but gave up again. I learned to be an electrician
at the O.R.T.*

When I asked him what his life was like when he first
arrived in the U.S., Simon explained:

*I had tracked down an uncle in America who sent me
an affidavit. I thought that he owned a button factory in
New York. He was, however, a workman in a belt factory.
I vowed that within 10 years I would be independent
and rich. At the beginning I lived with my uncle in
Brooklyn. He was a very pious man, unlike myself. On
the first Rosh Hashanna at the synagogue, my neighbor
suddenly leaned over and said, "You are not praying
either; let's go to the movies." We left at once. From that
day on we became inseparable. He, too, was a camp
survivor.*

*One month later he left his sister and I left my uncle
as we found a small apartment in Brighton Beach near
New York. We held various jobs and were always able
to manage our money. When I earned $35 a week, I
adjusted my way of living to my income. I never felt
poor. I worked in hotels during the summers, earning
$10,000 a season. This procured me the means to attend*

school full-time. I passed all grades from 9th to 12th in one and a half years and graduated proudly.

My friend and I became salesmen in a large fabric store. There, we specialized in curtains and became excellent advisors in curtain-making. One day, we decided to use our know-how to open our own curtain store. We used to give estimates for hotel and office construction sites that had huge bay windows. I was in charge of administrative matters. My partner cut the curtains. My mother, who had arrived two years after we started the business, sewed the material until we were able to hire seamstresses.

Not wanting work to be the most essential part of our lives, we worked only five days a week and took long vacations in the summer and winter. We had learned during the years of deportation that is was useless to work yourself to death. Money is only worth what you make of it. When you earn too much you are sure to lose it all. This had happened to my father.

We eventually accepted a third partner, Marc, who was a former inmate of Taverny, and today we are one big family. When one of us goes away, the others take care of his children.

On becoming a U.S. citizen, Simon recalled:

I vividly remember my naturalization ceremony. All emigrants who had arrived in New York five years earlier were present at this almost religious ritual. The judge presiding at the ceremony had also come as an emigrant. He said that we were all equals now, full-fledged citizens of the United States. I consider myself an American but all my friends are Jews. Ten percent of my income is distributed to the poor, 90% of which goes to Jewish charity and 10% to non-Jewish welfare organizations which assist starving children in Biafra or Cambodia. I am deeply concerned about hungry children, whoever they may be.

After filling out the forms for German compensation payments, I was summoned by a German psychiatrist.

When he requested that I describe life in Auschwitz, I answered very calmly, "Every morning the SS served us orange juice for breakfast." He was very annoyed and reprimanded me. I flew out in a rage. He knew perfectly well what had happened in Auschwitz! Of course, I wasn't granted any compensation payment, but I don't regret my fit of temper or my aggressiveness. I have overcome my hatred for the Germans. Since that time I have realized that not all of them are the same. There is the older generation and there are those who were born after the war. It is not right to generalize. Still, I never buy any German products, nor do my children. I have never set foot on German soil. I am reluctant to leave the security of the United States.

I have been to Israel, though, and was shocked at the low level of Jewish culture there. A Jew has to be aware of the laws even if he is not living a religious life. My children were raised according to these principles. I sent them to Jewish schools because I wanted them to understand. I wanted them to feel at ease when with pious Jews, like my uncle and my mother, but they are free to choose their own way of living.

Simon's son, listening in on our conversation, told me at a later date that he had resented his father's strict education. Compelled to go to the synagogue twice a month, he would spend his time chatting with others, just as his father used to do. Though he thoroughly disliked the religious studies, he has changed his mind about them for he can now move without compunction among Orthodox Jews. He was recently engaged to a young religious Jewish girl and, once married, they will live a Kosher life.

Simon continued his story:

As far as I am concerned, I do not believe in God. If he really exists, he should be denied and shunned. I continue to go to the synagogue each Friday and am an active member of the Jewish community. Once a year, when monies are collected, I stand up to make a speech. I don't find it an easy task, yet we take in twice as much money when I am the speaker. I usually tell the congregation: "What good is money to you? My father had a lot of money too, but the Germans took everything away from him. You have been spared only because you happened to be here. You might have been in Europe like your brothers just as well."

I saw Holocaust; *I agree with Elie Wiesel when he says that too much has been said about the Jewish people allowing themsleves to be led like sheep to be killed. It is true, unfortunately, that the Jews did not put up any resistance but that was the fault of their rabbis. Once, in the ghetto, my brother and I wanted to buy arms like many others. Our fathers asked the rabbis' advice and were told: "If you buy arms you'll endanger us, and the Germans will retaliate. Don't do it." I am terribly upset about their ignorance.*

I really dislike remembering the past. After my arrival in the United States, and once I had learned to speak English, I used to meet Europeans who constantly spoke about the war and the camps. It upset me very much as it was contrary to my philosophy—always forge ahead. This is why I decided to marry an American girl.

Nevertheless, deportation definitely plays an important role in my everyday life. I never make any long term projects. The only things that are important to me are being independent and living one day at a time.

Marc—We Want You

At the time Marc arrived at Taverny, his growth appeared to have been stopped by the war. Now, however, he looks like a typical American: tall, slim, smart-looking and elegant. He speaks English perfectly with no trace of an accent. Although he is more reserved than his friend and partner Simon, he still agreed to speak:

I was born in Hungary in 1929. I was the only member of my family in the camp. I would not have wanted to be with a father or brother as I would have had to share my bread or soup with him. I worked in a coal mine. I only

80

survived because I minded my physical hygiene.

In Taverny, I received an affidavit and a ticket from an aunt in New York. When I arrived at her house she told me that two of my brothers were still alive in Italy. Had I known about this before, I would have certainly joined them. Because she was childless, my aunt had purposely kept the information from me.

I was very unhappy. I immediately found work in a tie factory, but I was 16 years old and led a very dull life. Then, one year later, I signed up for the U.S. Army. I had the tattooed numbers removed from my arm and adopted an American name. I was the youngest officer in the United States and they chose my photo for the recruitment posters of the U.S. Army: a large poster saying, "We want you!"

I felt at ease at last. I knew where I belonged and I started growing again.

I stayed in the Army for four years, where I received letters from an American woman who was a friend of Simon's wife. I made her acquaintance after four years of correspondence. We became engaged and were married soon after. My young wife did not want me to sign up for another six years in Oklahoma, so Simon employed me. I became a salesman for him and we later became partners. I do a lot of travelling. Right now, I go on business trips to Saudi Arabia and third-world countries. I have been very successful on these trips and we obtain most of the orders from those countries.

I never tell anyone that I am a Jew and that I have been in the camps for it is useless and I don't want people to feel sorry for me. When I travel with my children to Israel, though, I take them to Yad Vachem, the holocaust museum. It is the best of its kind.

Not a day goes by that I don't think of the camps. I have learned three lessons: first of all, to know people and myself; then, to detest the Germans—we never buy any German products; and finally, in camp I vowed never to yield, never to be caught.

At the moment of liberation I felt sure that nothing of

*the sort could ever happen again, but I am not as con-
vinced of it anymore. I went to see my brothers in Israel
in 1973. Both are career officers. I went with them to
Naplouse. They lent me a gun, but I had mixed feelings
about carrying it; I was proud and ashamed at the same
time. In my opinion, the Arabs should recoup some ter-
ritory. Anyhow, Israel will be unable to keep it all.*

Marc was very young when he had been deported. Out of
a sense of self-preservation, he denied his past, constantly
searched for a protective social sphere, and appeared strong
and well-balanced.[1]

But without generalizing, can anybody actually recover
from such a childhood, such an adolescence?

Eugene—Nothing to Reproach the Germans

In Taverny, Eugene had been the life and soul of the
home and proudly recognized himself playing the accordion
in the photos I had brought to New York. As a taxi-driver,
he declared that his car was the only place where he could
talk. He kept watching the road and gave me the "$200 tour"
as he revealed his life story to me. Born in Hungary of rich
parents, he was deported to Yavichewitz where he worked
in the coal mines. At the time of liberation he was staying at
barracks 66 of Buchenwald:

*The barracks was divided into two sections: on one
side were the Polish, protected by Gustave, the head of
the block. On the other side were Hungarians and
Rumanians, those he unscrupulously sent to death when
young people were called for. I found my brother in
Buchenwald after the liberation. He wanted to return
home but I didn't, for I was afraid of the communists.
He left me behind feeling no remorse even though I was
14 years old at the time, one year younger than he. I'll
never forgive him. I hate him and never want to see him*

---

[1]Freud A. The Ego and the Mechanisms of Defense, New York, Inter. Univ. Press,
1964, page 72.

again. He sold all of our family belongings and kept all of the money for himself. He later went to Israel and only wrote to me when he was short on money. He is now living in Munich and is very rich. The other day he called me from there, just to brag about having the means to make long distance calls. I told him that I never wanted to hear from him again.

Eugene spoke to me about the children's homes:

We behaved like maniacs when we arrived at Ecouis. I think that the pious ones, especially Moshe, really had some nerve to demand Kosher food. Running through the countryside all day I saw poor French peasants with nothing to eat, while we were fed lavishly. It was disgusting to hear the religious ones ask for Kosher meat and special things. When the pious group left for Ambloy, I decided not to go along and went to several Buchenwald homes in Paris. But they were so messy and there was absolutely no discipline; I didn't like it at all.

One day I met Gabor, a Hungarian I knew from Ecouis, who told me: "Come with me to Taverny, you'll see it's nice there." So, I went. I felt at home right away even though I wasn't that pious. Because of you, the home was well run and disciplined, and everyone was kept busy.

I really liked it in France and deeply regret leaving there. As you can see, I now speak French. I used to have a great time in Paris, but you didn't know about it. I had a girlfriend there who went back to her family in England. So, when I obtained an affidavit and an American visa in 1948, I decided to give it a try in the New World. Oh, I didn't think that the money was lying around in the streets of New York, but I thought life would be easier there than it was in France.

The poorest of my three aunts was the most helpful— she cooked my favorite dishes—but the other two were constantly afraid I would ask them for money. I got the message; I never set foot again in the rich aunts' houses and I was too embarrassed to go to the poor one too often.

I finally found a job with a German-Jewish butcher. He was a great old man who treated me like a son. I worked six days a week from early morning 'til late at night, never receiving a penny of pay, but he was extremely good to me! I stayed with him for 22 years, until he died. His son took over the business but I didn't want to work for him because he ordered me around.

After that, I bought a taxi and a license. I was too busy to go to evening classes, so I ended up learning English from the other taxi drivers. I am on my own. I don't want to work for a company. We independent cab owners help one another. I have an intense dislike for the others—the drivers of white-roofed cars. I work mostly in the afternoons and evenings and sleep until eleven in the morning. I have rented a lovely apartment in the Bronx. I often see Meyer, Daniel's younger brother.

I try not to think of the camps; I want to forget. Why talk about it all the time? I frequently carry German tourists. They are very proper and kind and pay large tips. I explain the sights of New York to them in German. When they ask me where I learned their language, I tell them that I was a "Kriegsgdfangener" (prisoner of war). I cannot blame them—they just obeyed orders. But I really came to hate Hungarians during the war. They have cruel eyes and they hate Jews. They'd kill any Jew they came across. I can smell their presence. I refuse to carry them in my cab.

The other day, while buying a take-out meal in a Jewish restaurant, I noticed that the owner's number was very close to mine. I asked him, "Leon—doesn't that remind you of something? Marek—remember?" He almost fainted. I had been right, we were together in the mines and the barracks. He served me a triple portion and I said to him, "It's not now that I need it. I could have used it in Yavichewitz!" I go back to that restaurant every week and, of course, we chat.

84

Eugene invited me to a Jewish restaurant for lunch. Despite his cockiness, he seemed very shy and lonely. He was only 13 when he arrived at camp. He remembered his parents well. His character was just starting to develop at that time. He adjusted quickly to life in concentration camps, realizing the importance of being resourceful. He acted like an adult then, but when life returned to normal, he lost his self-assurance and his social standing crumbled to pieces. He has since become a shy, insecure and unhappy man. He feels left out and was unable to find someone to marry. He currently has a widow friend whom he "pampers and spoils" with hopes that one day "she'll agree to marry him."

Having been deported at a time when his character had not yet hardened, when his mind was not yet critical enough to judge his social environment, he was deeply marked by his past experiences and will remain a "survivor" all his life.

Meyer—Habit and Regret

Meyer, the younger brother of Daniel, who has become a physicist, took care of his older brother in camp and in Taverny: "He reflected and I acted. He used to say: 'We will not make it.' But I would look around and detect a piece of bread. I was always there when something was handed out. I learned to survive in camp."

At age 49, Meyer is shy and indecisive. He said that the only time he thinks about the camp is when other people talk about it:

At those times, memories return to me and I have trouble sleeping. I become restless and nervous. I only watched part of the movie Holocaust *because the movie was not realistic—I was there and I might say that it was completely wrong. I am sure that no one would have watched it if they had portrayed what really happened there and had shown the great mass of corpses. As far from reality as it was, it still had a tremendous*

85

impact on non-Jews. On the days it appeared on televi-
sion, my hairdresser closed shop early so that he would
not miss the beginning of the movie.

I was 14 years old at the time of liberation. I was very
small and didn't understand what was going on. For
me, it meant that there was suddenly bread to eat. I went
to Weimar to steal a bicycle—it was the first bicycle to
be brought to Buchenwald and I constantly watched it. I
once needed to blow up the tires and asked a Ukrainian
for his pump. In return he wanted me to let him take a
short ride. He never came back.

Meyer only kept vague memories of Taverny but is very
grateful to France and the O.S.E. for having offered a home
to the children of Buchenwald:

Those who were not able to leave the camps at that
moment and stayed in Germany started dealing in the
black market. They continued this kind of life afterwards
because they did not have the chance to slowly adjust
that we had through living in a children's home and
receiving an education.

Living in New York in the house of a very poor aunt, he
held several jobs. He studied simultaneously, first at the
yeshiva and then at the university. He managed to rent a
small apartment and go to evening classes, passing all ele-
mentary and high school grades, and went on to a school
for electronic engineering.

After finishing school I was hired by a manufacturer
of measurement instruments and still work for the com-
pany to this day. I work independently and come in
close contact with the customers. Without actually feeling
like an American, I have adapted well to life here. I am
no longer a practicing Jew, but I feel as Jewish as any
orthodox Jew. The friends I have, like me, were not born
in this country and we share a common past. I would
have liked to have married, but somehow I never had
the courage to go through with it. A young girl even

*came from Israel just to see me. . . . I changed my mind
at the last moment, though. I can't explain why I am
afraid of making final decisions, but I think the reason
lies in my past. I have often regretted never marrying. It
would have been nice to have had children. But I am an
old Jew now and am resigned to my fate. I am much
more at peace.*

*I am not really happy but I try to make the best of
things, although it isn't so easy. People here are under
pressure and I do not have much in common with their
way of living. I am sure people in Israel are much more
involved, as they are all Jewish and it is their own country.
I have seriously considered settling there, but I have my
job here and my habits are ingrained. It would be hard
to change. I have no worries about the future here. I
earn a good salary, I manage to save money, and I receive compensation payments from the Germans. I'll
always manage.*

Solomon—A 3880

Upon his arrival in New York, Solomon, now an important
surgeon, had the number which was tattooed on his arm
removed but he knows it by heart: A 3880. He was born in
1928 in Czechoslovakia and was the eldest of four children.
His mother, sister, brothers, and grandmother had been
taken away from the ghetto to unknown destinations. He
and his father were deported to Auschwitz:

*We stayed together for just a few days. I was sent to
Guisha, a small camp, where I had to work very hard
under the surveillance of young SS soldiers. We had to
unload cement bags weighing 200 pounds and carry
them along the road. When a prisoner collapsed, the
Kapos and SS soldiers killed him with heavy clubs. I
was unable to carry a 200 pound-bag by myself and hid
when the train with the bags arrived. I knew perfectly
well that I would be killed if I was discovered, but believed I had a better chance of survival by hiding.*

A year and a half after liberation, Niny met a Hun-

garian in London who was searching for the son of his friend—that son happened to be me. I was convinced that all my family had died. After reading the letter I had written to my newly-discovered parents, my mother fainted. I visited my parents in London and we quickly established the same excellent rapport we had before the war. Two days before the arrival of the Russians, my father had escaped with ten other prisoners into the forests in order to avoid being evacuated from Auschwitz to Buchenwald, thus escaping death.

I had received an affidavit from an uncle living in the United States and did not stay with my parents very long, but promised to have them join me there. I was able to obtain a Canadian visa for them; they settled in Montreal and are still living there. My uncle found work for me with a Hungarian Jew. I had to assemble cigarette lighters . . . I was very unhappy because I could not speak a word of English. I went to evening classes where, within one year, I learned to speak fluent English. With the help of scholarships, I studied to become an industrial engineer and graduated in Dallas. I had great difficulties finding a job that did not require me to work during Sabbath but I wanted to lead a religious life. Most of all, I wanted to become independent and decided to study medicine. It would not have been possible without my wife's help (she was a secretary at the stock exchange) years of biology, four years of medical studies, one year to specialize as a plastic surgeon—they were long and expensive studies. We waited until I held my diploma before having our first child. We now have two children who are very pious and receive a strict education.

My orthopedics and plastic surgery practice is going quite well. I have purchased the building where my offices are located and rent several offices for clinical purposes.

Is it a significant stroke of fate or just a coincidence? The only two survivors of Buchenwald who, to my knowledge, undertook long studies, have both found their parents again. The other is also a surgeon—in Paris.

Chapter Seven

New Options

Mr. Margulies—"As God is With us"

To this date, no commemorative gathering of the "former boys of Taverny," no wedding of one of their children is celebrated without Mr. Margulies. The former counselor still holds the same respect and authority he enjoyed during the days of Taverny.

One day in August of 1945, a huge furniture van arrived in Ambloy loaded with used clothing from American Jews. The children were anxious to exhange their striped pajamas for normal clothing, but Mr. Margulies pushed through the crowd, opened the doors of the truck and disappeared inside. Everyone silently accepted that he would be the first to select from the garments. A long time passed and Mr. Margulies did not reappear. The children grew impatient. When he finally emerged from the truck he said to the group, "I sorted everything according to size and category. Go in and help yourself." As for Mr. Margulies, he had kept his old clothing.

Mr. Margulies has not changed. In his modest apartment in north Manhattan, the religious section comprised of German Jews, he told me his story:

> *I was born in 1912 in Nuremberg, Germany. My parents were Polish. There were three children and my father was an invalid. My brother and sister succeeded in leav-*

ing for England before the war started, but I did not obtain my visa until 1939. I kept procrastinating about departing because I did not want to leave my father behind. Three days after war was declared, I finally decided to leave for Holland, which was a neutral country at that time, but it was too late. I was arrested at the border and taken to the prison of Nuremberg. From there I was deported to Buchenwald. Standing like my companions in the tightly packed train, I recited Isaiah's verse (VIII, 10): "They will form projects which will never be realized, they will draw up plans which will fail, for God is with us."

I was confined with political prisoners in Buchenwald, even though I had been arrested on the sole grounds of being a Jew. Political prisoners did office work in the camp, but I tried as best as I could to learn a trade and chose the most difficult but most valuable one—masonry.

It is most important for me to remain a devout Jew, to light the candles on Friday evening, to refrain from eating during fasting and to celebrate Jewish holidays. Other prisoners mentioned to me once how surprised they had been to see a tiny "sukkah" (shed) being erected in the camp court of the political section during the Feast of Tabernacles, and how much it had lifted their morale. Without the help of a calender, computing the exact dates of Jewish holidays was extremely difficult because they are determined by the lunar cycle. I got totally lost in my calculations for I did not know how many days were in the respective month, but each time a new transport of Dutch or Hungarian Jews arrived in camp, they gave me valuable information.

Despite the dangers involved, I needed to respect the commandments in order to identify with Judaism. Strange as it may seem, the Jewish "Kapos" were the ones who actually complicated our worshipping. Those in charge widely abused their authority; a foreman or head of barracks would frequently martyr a prisoner until he saw suicide as the only means of escape and jumped into the electric fence that surrounded the camp. Most of the Jewish Kapos disregarded all Jewish traditions. When prisoners said their prayers, the Kapos slapped them and called them "Talmud." It was appalling to watch most of the prisoners surrender to the force of the most powerful.

Being pious saved my life one day, however. I had exchanged a few words with a comrade, which was strictly forbidden, and noticed the foreman putting my name in his notebook—an act which was usually followed by a death sentence. On the way back, a non-Jewish German and member of "The Friends of the Bible" told the foreman: "This man believes in the Bible," and my name was crossed out.

During camp life I realized how important it was to observe one's physical hygiene. Whatever the temperature, even if I had to break the ice, I washed my whole body in cold water every morning. I still do it now.

We heard what was happening several days before liberation from the political prisoners who listened to the radio and received newspapers. The American troops had advanced as far as 30 miles from Buchenwald and the Germans were resisting heavily. Not wanting a single prisoner to be alive when the Americans arrived, they decided to evacuate Buchenwald. The only free passage available was the road to the south, and they tried to remove all Jewish prisoners from the camp. But for once, the orders given by the SS were not obeyed; the political prisoners crossed their plans. My friend had procured other insignia than our yellow stars and we went into hiding, thus escaping the fate of the 26,000 Jews who died either in Dachau or on their way there.

Not more than two hours before liberation the camp was to be systematically destroyed. The Americans arrived on the 28th of Nissan (April 11), the exact date my oldest son was born many years later; to me this was a sign from God. In 1947, after Taverny, I joined my brother and sister in England. But when the Russians invaded Czechoslovakia in 1948, I panicked at the idea of a third World War and asked a friend of mine to send me *an affidavit for the United States.*

Since I was 36 years old when I arrived in the United States, I wanted very much to get married and have children, but I had to find work first. Convinced that the only way to be successful in America was to specialize in a field, I learned to be a cutter. I met and later married Ruth, who urged me to become an accountant for I was unable to earn enough money as a cutter. My wife and I run an orthodox home and our three sons are very devoted Jews. God is with us.

Naphtali—Well-balanced Again

The older brother of the little boy who protected his luggage with a toy gun in the port of Haifa in 1945 has become Consul General for Israel in an overseas country. Although he has no political affiliations, he initially accepted a government job in the Civil Service as assistant to Moshe Dayan, and then followed him to the Ministry of Foreign Affairs.

He said to me: "If you try to expose in your book that the sequels of concentration camp life forbade leading a normal life, you are certainly wrong as far as I am concerned." The account of his life demonstrates, however, that as for many of his comrades, his life would have taken another direction had the war not occurred.

His father had been great rabbi of the community of Piotrkow in Poland, where, out of the 60,000 inhabitants, more than 20,000 were Jewish. He had been an outstanding personality, the thirty-seventh descendant of a line of highly respected rabbis. A doctor of philosophy at Vienna University, he spoke several languages and had written innumerable articles and books. He had started writing his last book in 1935: an edict about the behavior under persecution and towards informers. Naphtali dragged the manuscript from one hiding place to the next, but in the end it got lost.

I was 13 years old when war was declared. I had four brothers, one of whom had left for Rumania shortly before the war. We met again in 1939 in an enclosed ghetto which no one was allowed to leave.

My father was aware of the looming danger and could have fled in time, but, as a rabbi, had the duty to remain with the members of his congregation for better and for worse. Between October 14 and 21st, 1942, 24,000 Jews from Piotrkow were herded into cattle cars. My mother went into hiding in a bunker with my little brother Lulek. My father refused to do so. He said that the Germans, not seeing the rabbi, would search all the bunkers and capture those who were hiding. He was deported with all the others, as was my elder brother. After this raid, all Jews who worked and lived on the outside like me were driven back into the ghetto. There were only 2,000 of us left, and the ghetto had become a camp enclosed by barbed wire. A collective kitchen was installed which was run by my mother.

We were deported to Germany in 1944, when the Russians approached our town. The men were taken to a camp near the border, the women further on to Ravensbruck. At the very last moment, I tore Lulek out of my mother's arms. He was seven years old and stayed with me at the camp installed for the Hassag Werke, a factory where they repaired tanks. I left him in the bar-racks when I had to leave for work. He was given the same food as everyone else, but from time to time people threw him some extra crumbs or peelings.

I have an optimistic temperament, and this did not change during deportation. Yet, I was sure I would never see my father or the rest of my family again. I am still not quite sure of what I felt then. I must have had a very lively imagination. What did I learn in the camps? I learned to survive!

At the time of the evacuation of Buchenwald, Lulek stayed in barracks eight with privileged senior inmates. From there, he was transferred to barracks 66 where Gustave, the head of the barracks, led a command of men whose mission was to punish informers by strang-ling them.

One week before liberation, the Germans assembled us two or three times a day for roll-call. The first time I went there I saw a friend of mine lying dead in a trench. Having no shoes of my own, I wanted to take his but I saw him stir very slightly and he whispered, "Lay down next to me."

Three days later I was brought out of the camp with other comrades and was taken to the train station. During the night, I jumped off the train with two others, but instead of hiding, I walked two nights in a row back towards Buchenwald for I did not want to lose Lulek. The Americans liberated the camp three days later. I contracted typhus and Lulek the measles.

Five weeks later, having recovered from their illnesses, they left for France. Naphtali wanted his little brother to gain back his strength before taking him to the Holy Land. Their father, mother and older brother had disappeared and finding their fourth brother, Chico, in Israel, was a great joy to them.

I volunteered for the Hagana and was first put through a training session. I would have liked to have entered the Hebrew University in Jerusalem, but gave up the idea because it was too far away and there were too many complications. In order to find a new peace of mind, I decided to study at a yeshiva and chose the one situated in the countryside, Peta 'h-Tikva; I needed to take long walks and be in touch with nature. At the beginning of my year and a half in this yeshiva, I reviewed what I had learned before.

I asked no one for help. During vacations I worked in the nearby orange plantations. I was not a typical yeshiva student—the kind who sits for hours at a time studying the Talmud. As a member of the Hagana, I participated in the illegal landing operations. I had completely adjusted to life in Israel. In fact, I did not see anything unusual in the way I had settled there.

At first, I thought that I had lost the best years of my life during the war. At age 22 or 23, though, I realized that I had far more self-assurance than other young people of my age, due to my experiences in the camps and my clandestine activities.

I waited to get married until 1956 when I reached financial independence working as a journalist. My wife and I have four children and I feel very close to them. My youngest son often visits his uncle Lulek who talks more freely about the past than I do; when he returns from his visits he frequently asks me to confirm certain incidents.

Naphtali's wife told me how sick he became while covering the Eichmann trial as an official journalist. He was haunted by nightmares and needed to seclude himself in total silence. She sought the advice of a psychologist, who suggested that he see some of his former inmates. Talking about the camps did, indeed, make him feel better again.

Naphtali believes that he is leading a completely normal and satisfying life in the Holy Land. Still, at times, he admits to feeling somewhat different from the others:

Other people make plans, strive for success, while I have the impression that I have achieved more than I could ever have hoped for, and I will undertake nothing to improve my situation. I believe that I am the only person in Israel who has never asked for an increase or a bonus. I am happy with what I have. I do, at times, think about getting a promotion, but would not take great pains to obtain one. I have been successful in my job because I conscientiously carry out the tasks given to me as my parents taught me to do. My children, true to the religious tradition of their forefathers, display the same attitude. This is most important to me.

I believe that being older than his comrades and having been exposed to his father's influence helped him find a new peace of mind.

Alex—A Sheep in the Army

Alex was 15 years old when he arrived in Taverny, but he

looked more like 12. On Sabbath, we asked him to sing "Shaeffele," a Yiddish song about a shepherd who lost his sheep but recovered them with the help of God. We ended up calling him "Shaeffele," and, in fact, no one remembered his true name.

I met up with him accidentally in Tel-Aviv. A tall man with blue eyes and white hair came up to me and asked me if my name was Judith. It was Alex. We sat down to chat and he opened up freely, "so that no one ever forgets."

I was born in Rumania in 1930—the youngest of eight children. My parents were already 45 years old at my birth. My mother was a holy woman. We were very poor, but none of the beggars who knocked at our door were ever sent off empty-handed. Our house was spotless and sparkling clean. Even the two-handled bowl filled with water with which we used to wash our hands before meals was polished and shining at all times. Thanks to these hygienic practices, I was able to survive the camps. I constantly tried not to dirty myself and washed in cold water every morning.

We spoke Yiddish and Rumanian in our family and I studied at the heder. When war broke out, everyone was first confined to a ghetto. Then, all the Jews of our little town, 50 percent of the population, were sent to Birkenau-Auschwitz. I was separated from my family and sent to work at a construction site. It was very difficult work. Elie Wiesel, who I knew before the war, stayed with me the whole time. A German gave me the nickname "Der Kleine Trottel" (meaning little idiot, an expression that should not be taken literally though, as it often has a gentle connotation). He took quite a liking to me and gave me a piece of bread when I left for work every morning.

I was later put into barracks 66 in Buchenwald. When the Germans tried to make us leave the barracks three days before liberation, all of those who realized what was going on hid wherever they could. As for me, I sought refuge in the sewers under our barracks. I held onto a ladder for three days and nights, without food or water.

Every 20 yards there were ladders with other prisoners clinging to them. The Americans finally arrived and gave me a whole loaf of bread. Afraid that I wouldn't get any more, I saved part of it, an act which may have saved my life. Many others died from overeating. . . .

I remember the wonderful time in Ambloy and Niny who took me with her to the Bretagne, where she was in charge of a holiday camp. Shortly before leaving for the United States, I received a letter from my older sister, who had survived and lived in Antwerp, and without saying a word to anyone, I left to stay with her and her husband. She took care of me like a mother. While in Belgium, I gave up the idea of leaving for America and joined the Betar, a very nationalistic Jewish Youth Movement. I hoped to participate in the struggle for the creation of a Jewish country. At age 17 I embarked on the famous "Atalena," the ship which carried arms for the Irgoun, a clandestine radical movement, and was later sunk on Ben-Gourion's orders outside of Tel-Aviv.

Eager to fight for my country, I volunteered for a combat unit shortly after I arrived in Israel. Once in the army, I started growing like a mushroom and am now over six feet tall. I kept to myself and did not search for my comrades of Taverny. I would go to Tel-Aviv during leave, buy a pita-falafel (a pancake stuffed with chickpea balls) and a bottle of soda, and sit on a shaded bench on Rothschild Boulevard. I was happy. I would return to my quarters in the evenings.

The Military Police was instituted two years after I had become a soldier. They recruited all tall men and I, of course, was one of them. I stayed with them until I retired at age 52, having slowly moved up the ladder until I became a colonel.

When I was 23 years old, I met a woman soldier of Rumanian origin who had not been deported, and I married her. She is a nurse now. Her parents, especially her mother, are very nice to me. We have two children— a son who works at the Ministry of Defense, and a daughter who is married. I never speak about the camps to them, but they know everything for they have read every book on the subject. I realize that I over-react with them—I am too affectionate. My daughter, who lives close by, recently had a baby. Once a day my daughter calls and says, "Papa, I just prepared the baby's bath." At that point I drop everything and run over there. I hold my grandchild's feet and am overwhelmed with happiness.

I tried to suppress the past for a long time. The only item I saved are the pants I wore when I was deported. I cut off the legs to make gym shorts out of them. I was about to throw them away when they became too tight, but remembered that they were the only ties to my parents that I had left, so I kept them. I wash them myself and never show them to anyone.

Yes, the past, of course, is constantly on my mind. I have nightmares and think of my parents more frequently than before. Now that I can afford it, I wish I could spoil my mother and repay her just a little for the sweetness and kindness she brought into my life.

I am content with my life. At the time of liberation, I never would have thought that I would reach my present position. I have been in charge of the military prisons. This may seem strange considering my past, but because of my past experiences I always made efforts to ease the prisoners' lots. Whenever I proposed a mitigation of penalty, my request was given consideration.

I have not left Israel since I arrived here in 1947. Three years ago, the army sent me to the NATO countries to study the methods of various military prisons. Well aware that Germany was a member of NATO, I was very reluctant to go and consulted a rabbi who told me: "This trip is part of your duties, you have to go." All went well until I arrived in Germany. I was terribly scared and asked for an interpreter at the Israeli Embassy. German officers lined both sides of the staircase leading to their offices. Sweat poured over my face; without the company of the interpreter I think I would have fainted. When it was over, they asked me to sign their guest register. Most of my predecessors had written: "Thank you very much. Everything was perfect." I just wrote in Hebrew: "I heard your explanations." The official part of my job was over. One of the German officers, having heard the translation of my comment from the interpreter, said to me: "You have been such an attentive listener that I believe that you understand German very well." The interpreter translated my answer from Hebrew: "That's right, I understand German perfectly well." "But why did you ask for an interpreter then?" retorted the German officer. I rolled up my sleeve exposing my camp number and, forthwith, a chorus of voices exclaimed: "But we had nothing to do with it! We are much too young, it was the other generation!" They asked where they could take me and I answered: "Zum Bahnhof" (to the station). By the time I reached Paris where I met my wife, I was completely shattered.

I am no longer practicing the Jewish religion. I do not believe that God is concerned about humanity. Still, I am convinced that a core of devout Jews must carry on the past, as they will perpetuate Jewish traditions. While in the army, I fought for the exemption of yeshivoth students from military service.

"Shaeffele" was one of the lost sheep who found a new shepherd—Israel—and who received compensation for his forever lost youth—his granddaughter.

Chapter Eight

Paris is Not Far From Taverny

An Unwanted Mother

Too young to learn a trade, many of the little boys of Taverny returned to France to go to school and to learn French. Often, they decided to settle in France. I discovered four of them in Paris: Bernard and Victor, two brothers, and Jacques and Michel, two friends who had been inseparable since liberation. Upon his arrival at Ecouis, Michel was eight years old and Jacques, ten, but they were both as small as five-year-old children.

Michel was three years old when the ghetto he was living in was evacuated. While he was staying at Ambloy, a telegram arrived from the German Red Cross stating: "Have just found Michel's mother. She'll arrive tomorrow." The child remained impassive at this news and his comrades lacked enthusiasm as well. When asked why their attitudes were such, they explained: "No one really believes that it is Michel's mother. He cannot remember her, and we don't believe that she is still alive." Nevertheless, on the following morning, Michel went to the station with a group of his comrades to wait for his mother and the woman did arrive.

A strange atmosphere prevailed that evening despite the festive table we had prepared for dinner. Michel listened silently to the stories his mother told him about the ghetto. She hugged and kissed him, put him to bed and sat at his bedside until he fell asleep. On the following morning she declared that she had to catch the first train to Paris—that

101

she had to go on errands. I got up to pack Michel's suitcase, but she stopped me and said: "No, don't bother. He'd only be in my way. I'd prefer to leave him here."

I realized that the children had instinctively been right. Having been a friend of Michel's family, this woman had used the opportunity to get out of Germany. Michel met her again in the United States many years later. Not at all blaming her for the role she had assumed, he became a close friend of hers for she was the only person who had known his family—the family forever lost to him.

Michel is now in the advertising business and lives in Paris. He married a non-Jewish girl whom he met at Club Méd. Their two little boys are blond and blue-eyed like their mother.

Michel explained to me that he owed three things to his wife: his driver's license, which he finally obtained, after many vain efforts, once he was married; the courage to buy an apartment; and his sons.

In their large living room, family photos ("My family," Michel's wife pointed out) are hanging side-by-side with an engraving of the Wall in Jerusalem where Jews say their prayers ("Michel's family," she said).

"Be Quiet, My Child"

As for Jacques, he retraced his family. He was in Versailles when he was informed by the O.S.E. that his mother had survived and was living with her two daughters in Munich. Having learned a lesson in the case of Michel's supposed mother, we decided not to have her come to us, but to send Jacques to her during summer vacation. The trip was a great trial for him. Since he did not remember his mother, he had no idea how to behave. He felt at ease with her when he arrived in Munich, yet his anguish persisted. Only during Sabbath, when his mother lit the candles and prepared the traditional dishes, did the memory of his childhood and the mother he had lost, return to him.

Jacque's mother later came to France through the O.S.E. with one of her daughters. The two women worked as seamstresses making skirts in a tiny room. At night the young girl studied for her diploma. Once he was able to afford it, Jacques rented an apartment for his mother. He invited me to her place one evening and asked her to sing for me. She sang a song in Yiddish that contained the following words: "Be quiet, my child. If the Germans hear you cry, they'll find us and we'll all be killed. Hush, hush, my child."

One Yard of Bread

Michel needed a dialogue with Jacques in order to open up and reveal his past to me:

Michel: *I was born in Piotrkow, Poland, where we lived next door to the rabbi. Lulek, his youngest son, was the same age as I. We both worked in the glass factory which the Germans had opened in the ghetto. We were four years old and had to bring water to the glass-blowers who were always thirsty. The factory stayed open night and day and the crew worked in eight-hour shifts. When night came and I was unable to keep my eyes open any longer, I would build a shelter out of empty boxes and fall asleep. The German guards always found me and threw buckets of cold water on me to wake me up. Lulek and I met again in Buchenwald. He saved his brother's life a few days before liberation by hiding him in our barracks.*

Jacques: *I had also hidden under a mattress with my father. He died shortly after liberation.*

Michel: *I wasn't staying with my father, but managed to see him every evening. It gave me a sense of security.*

Jacques: *Which barracks was he in?*

Michel: *Number 62. I stayed there for one week; people died there every night. Then, he was transferred to a stone barracks and I to number eight. You and your father were in barracks 66. I was only eight years old but I remember very well. A child of eight during that period was the same as a 20-year-old boy today. The only thing I knew when we were liberated is that*

103

one could die of hunger.

Jacques: *On liberation day, I heard shots and executions on the outside and a different siren than on other days. People said, "That's the Americans. They're going to parachute breads one yard long." I looked up to the sky, searching for the bread.*

I often wondered whether it would not have been better for the little ones to have stayed with a family rather than in a children's home, and questioned Jacques and Michel.

Jacques: *Not necessarily. I think that people would have thought concentration camp children to be weird. Slipping all sorts of food into their pockets while there was enough to eat would not have been accepted as a reflex action by those who had never lived in the camps. Being among peers at least gave us a sense of security. Niny mentioned to me once that we did not know how to play, that we were just sitting around all day as if we were feebleminded. At least we were all alike—we did not differ from the others.*

Michel: *We did not speak a word of French during the first few months and were fortunate to have a very gentle teacher at our school, Mademoiselle Lacroix. I made 74 mistakes in my first dictation and there were only 74 words in it.*

Jacques: *The period of adjustment lasted a year or two. We learned to speak French well, and in the company of others, we became children again.*

Michel: *I remember my Bar-Mitzvah in Versailles. I received a watch and roller-skates as gifts. I tried out my roller-skates the next day, fell, and broke my watch. People in France thought that only small children lived in the homes, and I inherited all the shoes they sent. I owned 17 pairs and took them along from one home to the other. Shoes are very important to a Jew. I was also given a huge pair of pants in Ambloy.*

Jacques: *What Michel said is true: to a Jew, shoes are the most important thing. I am terribly scared that our little boy might lose his shoes. I once woke up with a*

104

jolt during a vacation, because I was afraid that I had lost my son's shoes.

Being able to communicate—in French—gave Jacques and Michel a sense of security, and they never again thought of settling elsewhere than in France. But they still suffered the sequels of deportation; neither of them had integrated into French society and, as a result, felt isolated in Paris. At least Jacques had his family: a mother, a sister, and brothers-in-law. As for Michel, he had adopted all his former comrades of the Buchenwald group as his family.

Bernard and Victor—A Deeply Buried Past

Bernard was 12 years old at liberation, his brother Victor, 15. Bernard very emphatically explained to me that he never speaks of his past. He works for a large home appliance company in Paris and is quite content with his job. A large portion of his library contains documents about World War II, but he keeps his own story to himself.

Victor, however, did reveal a few hidden memories. He said that he often thinks about his mother, an unusual woman, who was deported with his little sister. His mother could have escaped from the ghetto, but unable to abandon her old mother who lived with them, she decided to stay. Victor spent ten long years becoming a locksmith. "One year in a camp was the equivalent of ten years!" he said. He and his brother sailed together on the Exodus to Haifa and back to Europe, landing in Marseille shortly before the proclamation of the state of Israel.

I was seventeen and a half years old then. Since I was of age to become a soldier, they offered to take me back to Israel, but not my brother, who was too young to travel. I told them: "During all the years in camp I took care of my brother, and now you want to separate us? I am not going to leave!"

In 1956 he married a young girl of French origin whose parents had also been deported, and he assumed French nationality. He is a devout Jew, and is very concerned about giving his children a feeling of security—the security that he had not known as a child. In order to preserve his peace of mind, he has deeply buried his past and the only after-effect of camp life he ever talks about is his brother's stomach ulcer.

Survivors of Buchenwald are a minority in Paris, where society dislikes the unusual element. There is no doubt that Bernard and Victor refused to speak about their past out of a subconscious sense of self-protection. They associate very little with other people, who, knowing very little about them, cannot detect anything unusual.

Chapter Nine

Fighting For Us: Israel

Martin—A Baffled Vengeance

Martin's face contrasted strangely with the pale complexion of the other boys of Taverny: his cheeks were round and red like a little farmer boy's. His healthy looks had caused him to receive even smaller rations than his comrades in Buchenwald. He had come to the camp of Yavichewitz at age 13 and was required to work at sorting out coal, standing for 12 hours at a time without resting. His father worked in the coal mines in the same camp until he collapsed one day and was exterminated. One Sunday, the SS carried a cartload of green, rotten bread out of the kitchen. One of the prisoners walked over to it and the others followed. To the little boy he was then, the big cluster of men fighting for bread, that, in his home town would have been fed to the pigs, was a horrible sight. He swore never to become like those poor, famished creatures:

> *Chubby-cheeked as I was, I never received an extra piece of bread and soon became a "Moslem." If I pushed the skin of my feet with my finger, a dent would remain for at least one hour. A Czechoslovakian doctor told me: "You need vitamins, but I don't have any." So, my feet remained covered with red and black spots and I continued to drag myself to work.*
>
> *To this day, I don't understand how I was able to run to the gate when the Americans arrived, as I wasn't even*

able to walk at the time; but their presence seemed to heal me. I was still terribly bitter, though, and was sure that the whole world would rise to avenge those who had suffered in the camps. But the Americans protected the German soldiers, bringing them food as if they were babies and scolding us when we spat at them. The Jews among the American soldiers were taken away from Buchenwald, and it made me understand that a fraternity exists, or rather different fraternities exist: those among Jews, and those among non-Jews.

Having heard from Arie, who had always worked with me at sorting coal, that there was a country of Jews called Palestine, I decided to learn a trade, to live there, and to fight for the country. I chose carpentry as a trade for the following reason: I remembered a sickly boy of my age who lived in my home town of Hungary; his mother made him work for a carpenter. He had to gather big boles of trees from the forest, cut them up and make objects out of them. He became a tall and strong boy. When he was in our gang, the non-Jewish boys were afraid of him, but to me he was an ideal.

Martin tried to leave for Palestine as quickly as possible, but despite his desire to be active and to fight, Mr. Margulies held him back, not wanting him to leave without a visa. Mr. Margulies was able to obtain two in 1946, one for Arie and one for Martin.

In the meantime, an astonishing incident had occurred. Martin had been invited to lunch in a restaurant of the Rue des Rosiers.[1] Some Jewish women dining there, who knew that he had survived Buchenwald, came over to him and asked him whether it was true that there was almost nothing to eat in the camps. He answered, "Yes, it is true," and they started crying. Martin thought:

---

[1]This was the famous Goldenberg Restaurant in the Marais section of Paris. On August 9, 1982, a bomb had been deposited there by anti-Semites. Six persons died, 22 were badly injured.

How can you explain what it means to be alone in the world, to have lost your parents, seven brothers and sisters, and to find out that people's only worry was whether you had enough to eat? At that time, I decided never to mention it to anyone again. Other people cannot understand. That is how I cut all links to the past.

When, at age 18, he had at last arrived in Jerusalem, he went to all the carpenters in town and asked the best among them to hire him. When asked, "Do you know that I only pay two pounds a week? Can you live on that?" Martin's response was, "Did I ask what my salary would be? All I want is to work here."

Martin's dream was to live in a village, but when his dream did not materialize, he entered the Navy. As a frogman, he was just about to sign up for a mission when his companions asked, "As a practicing Jew, won't there be a problem when you have to go on a mission during Sabbath?" Martin told me:

I had felt like a brother to them. I was deeply hurt and didn't sign up. I thought that I would have to try something else. I returned to Jerusalem and worked as a carpenter—not because I wanted to become rich, but because I wanted to be independent and make enough money to marry and have a family, which I did when I was 35 years old.

Martin dreamed about his family while in the camp. He continued to do so at liberation, and when no one came back, he was terribly downhearted. He confessed that he recently dreamed that he was repairing a room in his old family home. But instead of living in the good part of the house, he had stayed in the room he was working on. Suddenly, a stranger entered and his parents appeared at the same time. This dream had made him very happy. He'd had a similar, recurrent dream, but it only concerned the work he was doing; his parents had never appeared. Since then, he has realized that his trade represents a link to his childhood.

Martin ascribes his nationalistic convictions to his past despite his disappointment with the Navy. He said that he could hate neither the Germans nor the Arabs, but that he just wishes them "to be as far away as possible." Vengeance was not part of his plan.

Arie—Disenchantment

Arie's father, a prosperous grocery store owner of a small town in Ruthenia, was not a Zionist, but his much admired older brother had joined the Youth Movement of Bne-Aquiba. Arie followed his brother's example and became a passionate believer in the idea of the Holy Land.

One day I used all of my pocket money to buy a map of Palestine from a friend. My parents became frightened when the Germans occupied our town and asked me to give the map to them; I refused and took it to bed with me. That night, my father got hold of it and burned it. I'll never forget that incident.

The non-Jewish population of our town was very hostile. A boy threatened me one day and said, "You have killed my God!" One of the schoolteachers called a friend of mine a "dirty Jew." I was just a little boy of eight at the time, but I already knew the meaning of the word "anti-Semitism."

In April 1944, my whole family—my parents and their four children—was deported to Auschwitz. At our arrival there, Dr. Mengele sent my father to the left, where the gas chambers were located. I was about to follow him, but the doctor made me step to the right, even though I was small and very thin. The Germans beat us unmercifully, pushing us hard towards the barracks and bringing me to tears. Another boy, who was hardly older than myself, reprimanded me: "If you want to stay alive, stop crying and pull yourself together. You must be strong—despairing won't get you anywhere. See that you get a number tattooed on your arm and try to get out of Auschwitz as quickly as possible!" He appeared to me like a vision of Elias and, thanks to him, I regained

110

my self-control.

After having been transferred to Yavitchewitz, where he had to sort out coal with other young boys, Arie continued dreaming about Palestine and life on a Kibbutz, which he only knew of by hearsay. In his mind he saw a large "communa," a group of houses surrounding a wide yard: "Eretz Israel." The hope of living there some day sustained him, yet each detail of concentration camp life has remained engraved in his memory:

> *There were also non-Jewish Poles working in the camp's factory who, having heard that there were children among the prisoners, decided to share some of their more plentiful rations with us. The meat they gave us, however, was horsemeat. I couldn't eat it—it disgusted me—and I exchanged it for potatoes. This, by the way, saved my life: at the time of liberation we had not eaten for three days and were literally starving to death. The Americans gave us meat, but I was unable to swallow it and only accepted potatoes, which prevented me from getting sick.*
>
> *Some of the Germans were very sadistic, constantly inflicting new cruelties on us. One day, during an alarm, the electricity was cut off and a young Jew from our barracks seized the opportunity to escape over the otherwise electrified fence. He lived in the nearby forest like a wild animal, sneaking up to the villages during nighttime to steal food, but was recaptured soon after. The Germans interrupted our work and made us assemble in the large courtyard around the pole that held the gong which sounded morning reveille. There, we had to watch the hanging of the young fugitive. We were compelled to march past the dead body and repeat the phrase: "This is the punishment that awaits an escapee."*
>
> *The Germans debased and degraded us to a point where we lost all human dignity. One Sunday (our only day of rest), an SS soldier attached a piece of bread to the end of a string. He threw the piece of bread into the air and watched about a hundred prisoners jump up*

111

and down in attempts to grab the bread. To top it off, the soldier even set his shepherd dog against the poor, famished prisoners.

It was in camp that I decided never to live with non-Jews. My decision was confirmed by an incident that took place right after liberation from Buchenwald. A young communist had assembled all the children to make a political speech. He urged us to return to our country in order to partake in the communist movement. We continued to chat and he exclaimed: "What is going on here? Is this a synagogue?" This, of course, hardened our conviction not to comply with his request.

All of these memories came back to me at the time of the Eichman trial. It was during a military training period. A sergeant asked us to put the ammunition away after a maneuver. I heaved a box on my shoulders while many other soldiers just stood around talking. Noticing this, the sergeant exclaimed: "I can understand Eichmann. You are just a bunch of lazy no-goods." I let the box fall on the ground and blurted, furiously: "I've heard that somewhere before!" I complained to a higher ranking officer who made the sergeant apologize to me.

During the fights for the Old Town of Jerusalem in 1949, the Jewish soldiers had arrested a few Arabs from the Katamon section. They separated the men who were old enough to fight, from the women and children, grabbing one of the Arabs away from his youngsters who cried: "Papa! Papa!" Old memories surfaced and I had to turn away to hide my tears. Then, when I and a much older soldier were guarding Arab suspects, one of the prisoners asked to step outside to relieve himself. The soldier told him: "Do it here!" and I retorted: "You're armed, why not accompany him to the outside!" But he refused. Again, I felt sick and had to turn away to hide my feelings.

Being tubercular, Arie did not learn a trade in France. As soon as he was healed, he left for Palestine with his friend Martin. He was very downhearted when he realized that no one was going to pay special attention to him, be it in the home of Atlit, or in Tel-Aviv, or at the Agouda of Kfar-Saba where he had entered to join Martin:

I had gone to the Yeshiva Kol-Torah in Jerusalem, but I think it was a mistake. I joined the Hagana and the non-political Youth Movement, the Ezra. I wanted to meet as many Sabras (young, native Israelis) as possible. I was terribly lonely, though, until my brother arrived. He had also survived the camp. He intended to live in Jerusalem, which was still under British control at the time, but because of the unemployment situation there, had to go to Haifa.

I joined the Army because I wanted to participate in our fight for independence. The director of my yeshiva said to me: "All of your family has been exterminated. Shouldn't you try to stay alive?" But I replied: "The fate of my people is also my fate." I was shot in the lungs and stayed in a hospital for three months.

After his release from the hospital, Arie wanted to become a printer, hoping to receive an education and make up for the years he had lost. Seeing that there was a lack of teachers at the time, he attended a preparatory course and was sent to teach in a village school. Having to deal with undisciplined children and being extremely lonely, however, made it very hard for him. In 1954, at age 26, he married a Sabra of Russian-Polish descent. He started feeling better and tried to bestow upon his eldest son the many opportunities he had missed, convinced that the boy would make a brilliant career. But under the "influence of a friend," as he put it, his son had only money on his mind.

I think I am a better nationalist than other Israelis and that I am more critical of the shortcomings of my country. It is very important to continue evoking the deportations, however, on a more national dimension, by stressing the necessity of a State of Israel. It makes me very unhappy that my son wants to live in another country.

113

Since that time, his son has married and has become a store owner in Tel-Aviv.

After the war, thousands of survivors came to Palestine with the same convictions as Arie. According to statistics, one third of the population of Israel, about 20,000 people, were survivors at the time the state of Israel was founded. A majority of them believed that the deportations have created the need for a Jewish state. But today, Arie, and no doubt many of the others, are appalled at the deterioration of the initial ideal. Israel has become a State like many others.

Aron—A Heart of Stone

After receiving the news that his little brother Ouri was still alive in Germany, Aron immediately left Taverny to find him. They left together for Palestine as soon as they could.

Aron had been very happy as a child in Ruthenia (a former province of Czechoslovakia) and never dreamed of living anywhere else. But in 1941, his father joined the Hungarian army and was sent to the East. He never returned. The family ran out of money one year later, when Aron was 15. He left for Budapest to work with a trucker, who, having grown fond of him, let him share his apartment until the Germans occupied Hungary in 1943. Aron left him then and tried to cross over to Yugoslavia with a friend his own age, but was caught at the border and was sent to Auschwitz:

I was terribly shocked when I arrived at the camp and was furious at the leading Hungarian Jews, who must have known what was going but did not tell us. I was soon transferred to Magdeburg, another camp located close to a chemical factory. The prisoners had to accomplish the dirty work there. Food was insufficient in the camp. I wouldn't have survived had I not found ways to exchange vitamins from Red Cross supplies for bread or other food with privileged, non-Jewish prisoners in the "political" section. I was young then and the guards did not scare me. I was sure that once I had come out of this hell, everything would be the same as

114

*before: I would return to my home town, to my family
and my mother. I thought of nothing else.*

*Two months before liberation we were evacuated to
Buchenwald. I tore the yellow star off my uniform and
replaced it with a "T" (standing for Czechoslovakian)
and went into hiding until liberation. I was in a constant
state of terror. It was awful.*

The course of Aron's life underwent constant changes.
He embarked on the Exodus with his young brother, was
sent back to Hamburg where they spent three months in
another camp, and left once more for Israel with false
passports.

*I arrived in Israel during the Civil War and joined the
Army. I was a mine-clearing soldier, and was very happy
because we were no longer treated like sheep. We were
brave Jews defending our country.*

After leaving the Army, Aron worked as a mechanic for a
construction firm in Haifa. Once the project was finished,
however, he lost his job. He went to live in a home for
demobilized soldiers until he found a job in the port, setting
afloat a ship which was to bring new immigrants to Israel.
Once this job was complete, he was at a dead-end again.

*I was completely fed up with everything—not with
working 14 hours a day, but with the constant change. I
joined the police force and was very impressed by its
three-month training course. Our Scottish instructor in-
flicted British discipline upon us: properly made beds,
morning inspection. Even the manner in which we held
a fork was regulated. This kind of discipline had the
effect of a vaccination—it helped me accept the neces-
sities of life.*

Aron married and had two children, but it was not a
good marriage. His wife, not fully aware of the obligations
of a policeman, disliked his odd working hours. But, for the
children's sake, they refused to divorce. After ten years of

115

marriage, Aron left the police force and became a boat mechanic.

After ten and a half years, I realized that I had no future and was ready to give up. I wanted to be independent and opened a small pipe manufacturing company. This was shortly before the Six-Day War, at the height of the crisis. Of course, it didn't work out. I took a job in the factory where I work to this day. Everybody wants to be his own boss, but how does one do it?

Aron and his wife divorced a year and a half ago. His wife has since remarried. His sister-in-law, who does not approve of divorce, refuses to see him, thus preventing him from seeing his own brother. Aron is alone and unhappy. He continued:

I often suffer depressions like I did in Taverny. To get over them, I get in the car and drive to St. John of Acre. At times I can feel my heart—a heart that has become as hard as stone. Sometimes, it swells up and then shrinks again. It is very depressing. I haven't been to a doctor—I don't need one—I know what these crises are. I cannot stand anybody upsetting me or baffling my honor.

I never mention the past because I don't want people to feel sorry for me. But it's all the same, whether I talk about it or not; subconsciously, I am always thinking of the camps. I was very happy that Eichmann was caught. What a vengeance! I wish many more would be caught. I read every newspaper report about proceedings against Germans.

It seems to me that I lost the best years of my life in the camps. I was terribly frightened for my son during the Yom-Kippur War. I couldn't have endured to lose such a young son. Everyday I prayed to die in his place. I prayed to God not to let him die before he even had a chance to live. I am definitely in favor of peace, to the point of accepting compromises.

In the meantime, Aron has started to paint and has found

great relief in his new occupation. He paints the changing aspects of the sea, and has had some success with his paintings in exhibitions.

Aron bore a violent hatred within himself: hate against his own people for having made him a victim; hate against himself for not having resisted. Yet, in Israel, where he was given the opportunity to prove his strength by helping to build the new state, he has had less difficulty readjusting his life.

Chapter Ten

Safe at Last

Elie—Innocence

Elie was a quiet, gentle boy who had large, melancholic eyes. Because he was 14 years old when he arrived at Taverny, he was sent to school. He quit after the first day, however, and adamantly refused to go back. He was the son of a rabbi of a small Hungarian town. There were six children in his family. He and his older brother, Mendel, were the only ones to survive.

We never read the newspapers at home—we didn't get any. Yet, my father always knew what was going on and what lay in store for the Polish Jews. But he never thought that anything would happen to us.

The Hungarians arrested us one Sunday during the Jewish Passover, but we did not think it was serious. Each family was given a horse-cart onto which we loaded our belongings. We moved from place to place and at each halt had to leave some bags with our names tagged to them behind. Thirty-five days after we were arrested, the police ordered us to leave the remainder of our baggage. It was on Sabbath, but I did not have to follow the commandments for I was not yet 13 years old. I, therefore, took the responsibility of writing our new address on the tags that the police had given to us. We were then crowded into cattle wagons that had tiny, wired windows. What I remember most about our three-day journey

119

was the little baby in my mother's arms screaming for something to drink.

We arrived in Birkenau-Auschwitz in the evening and had to remain in the train for another night. On the following morning, prisoners in striped pajamas opened the doors. I was horrified at what I saw, yet, at the same time, was impressed by the terrific organization of the Germans. I remember a man named Dr. Fischer who held the same rank as Dr. Mengele. The two doctors watched the arrival of ten thousand Jews each day, never losing their good manners when greeting the new prisoners.

My father appeared before Dr. Fischer, who asked his age. Aware of what was going on, he answered: "I am forty-six years old but am still able to work." Dr. Fischer said to him: "Show me your hands," and, after inspecting them, sent him to the right. My brother, a very strong boy, was also sent to the right. Standing between the two, tightly holding onto their hands, I was able to slip through. The doctor said nothing.

We were sent to Yavichewitz to work in the coal mines. My father worked underground extracting coal. At the conveyor belt above ground, 42 children and adolescents had to clean the stones and dirt from the coal. It was far less straining work than that which my brother had to accomplish. One day, my father fell sick and Dr. Fischer promised to send him and the other sick prisoners to a hospital. We never saw our father again and never again mentioned him in our conversations.

Dr. Fischer was a very elegant man and often came into our barracks. He once distributed pills to the fourty-two children but we were afraid of being poisoned and refused to swallow them. Dr. Fischer very delicately picked a pill out of the box and swallowed it. This convinced us that they were, in fact, vitamins and we agreed to take them.

I met Martin, a Hungarian, who was my age and we occasionally recited the Guemara together. These were always very special days. Most of the time, however, I thought of nothing but food. One day, we received from Auschwitz some crusts of bread cooked in jam. They were so delicious that we planned to try the recipe after the war.

Mendel was quick to learn how to get along, but I was just a "schlemazal," a clumsy fellow. I stayed alive only because I was too young to do hard work and because we had a clean camp.

In 1945, as the Russians were advancing, the prisoners were evacuated from Yavichewitz and moved on foot to Buchenwald. Too weak to walk, Elie was carried by his brother during the long days of the march. They were separated, however, when they arrived in Buchenwald. The children's barracks seemed "good" to Elie. His daily rations consisted of just a half a pound of bread, instead of the full pound he received in Yavichewitz, but he did not have to work. He was glad that he did not have to leave the barracks, as "Buchenwald was such a large place." One evening, long after their arrival, someone entered the children's barracks and said to Elie: "Here is your brother."

He looked like a skeleton with eyes. I didn't recognize him. He was unable to see or to hear and was too thin to even sit down. He was working outside of the camp and unless he returned by six o'clock in the evening, he would be killed by the Germans. One evening, returning late to the barracks, he begged the Germans not to kill him. They hit him on the head with a big club and pushed him savagely through the gate; one of the prisoners helped him to our barracks. One of the boys had gone over to his parents' barracks and left a piece of bread that everyone craved on the table. The head of our table gave it to my brother. On the following day, one very exceptional boy went around to collect spoonfuls of soup for Mendel and ended up with a big bowl for him.

Mendel had to be hospitalized at the time of liberation and Elie, who had not seen him for some time, believed he was dead. But the boys were eventually reunited and left for

121

France together.

The castle of Ambloy, with its forty rooms, the park and lake at our disposal, was truly magnificent—a real paradise. We were very happy for we were allowed to do as we wished. I feel very sorry for myself when I think about what I had to go through, excluding my experiences at Ambloy.

After Easter of 1946, I went to the yeshiva at Aix-les-Bains where I met a group of boys from Taverny who were waiting to leave for Palestine. Recalling my father's love for the Holy Land, I decided to go there, too. I returned to Taverny for a few days to get my brother, but he refused to come along—he first wanted to become rich in America before following me to Palestine. I returned to Aix and we started off. At the end of a very, very long journey, we finally arrived safely at the Yeshiva of Gour in Jerusalem.

We were received at the yeshiva with open arms and our arrival was celebrated with a banquet. The directors of the yeshiva understood that we would not have been able to stand a separation and refrained from sending us to different families. They knew that we wanted to remain together and formed a special group at the yeshiva just for us.

The older students helped us catch up on the lessons we had missed. Because I was the youngest and had lost two or three years of studies, the teacher instructed me privately during the evenings.

The rabbi of Gour did not see me personally, but his spirit shed its light over all of us. We had the impression that we were fully understood even by those who had not been in Europe during the war. In the beginning, we talked excessively about the camps, evoking every single detail, every day of life there. Then, little by little, we refrained from mentioning the camps in our conversations.

When he was 21 years old, Elie met a young Hassidic girl born in Jerusalem. Because she held the same religious convictions as he and was a sweet and gentle girl, Elie married her.

Elie pretended to be of excellent health, although he was extremely lean and suffered from digestive orders. A recurring nightmare haunted him: he saw a man entering the barracks—his brother, Mendel—and although he had seen him two and a half months earlier, he did not recognize him.

The very young children seemed to have more difficulty recovering from their experiences than the older ones. Elie was 13 years old when he was deported. His mental development seemed to have come to a halt in Auschwitz. His only means of survival had been the protective shelter of law and order in the camp, which offered the same security he had known in his family. Psychological mechanisms of defense caused him to remember only the good incidents: the camp was clean; Dr. Fischer distributed vitamins; work was not too hard; the father's death was not mentioned; his brother was even given food after receiving a sharp blow on the head. Thus, everything seemed all right and life in the barracks was bearable.

Elie refused to admit that anything abnormal had happened to him. He pretended to be of good health and belittled his experiences by refusing to admit that the skeleton-like figure he saw in his dreams was his brother. Elie pretended to have found happiness in Gour, where he had been so well received. He had found a good wife there and was given a good job that suited his ever-innocent mind. All of these things speak of the heavy traumatic shock he had suffered.

His readjustment seems neither good nor bad. Anyway, what are the true criteria for a good readjustment? Reading Elie's story, one cannot help but weep over the million and a half Jewish children who were just as innocent as Elie, and who have disappeared.

Mendel—Growing Roots

Like his brother Elie, Mendel had no idea what was in store for him in Yavichewitz. He had to work very hard, much too hard for his young age, and, as a result, suffered great pain in his legs and feet.

I had been given two pairs of pants at camp. Elie had only one pair which was so large that he had to hold them up with both hands. I exchanged one pair of my pants for a leather belt that I gave to Elie to wrap around his waist, and a wooden spoon that he could use for eating soup.

My father, who always tried to obtain news about the events outside of the camp, was ridiculed by the other inmates, who often exclaimed: "All that counts in here is having thick soup." At first, I didn't understand what they meant by this, but I quickly became like the others— my only concern was to get enough food. I observed how men were reduced to the lowest level of debasement, how they became abject creatures who behaved like animals.

I was convinced that I would not be able to survive. At the time of liberation, I fell sick with typhus. The Hungarian doctor who treated me tried to convert me to communism and urged me to return to Hungary. Although I wasn't yet 17 years old, I refused to listen to him. As for the doctor, he returned to Hungary where he was sentenced to ten years in prison. . . .

I spent some time in a hospital when I first arrived in France and continued to get sick very often, even in Taverny. What was most bothersome, however, were the terrible nightmares that haunted me. I dreamt about a forest, about children who were going to be shot and whom we tried to hide. I used to wake up at night covered with sweat, and when the nightmares occurred during the day, I felt as if my head would burst.

In Taverny, Mendel only wanted to study the Talmud, but I insisted that he learn a trade and sent him to an electric shop. There, he was compelled to sweep the floors and go on errands. He came back after his first day and said to me: "Don't ever try to make me go back there. I am going to stay here and study." He became determined to "make a lot of money" and soon left for Antwerp, where he learned to cut

124

diamonds. By the time he had finished his apprenticeship, a severe economic crisis had broken out. "Why did I have to learn a trade that wasn't worth anything! This isn't for me after all!" he exclaimed. He returned to Taverny and asked an aunt in America to send him an affidavit.

Mendel's family in the United States received him with open arms and was very understanding. He entered a yeshiva in 1947 and two years later married a young girl he had met through his aunt. In 1953 he obtained a job as an instructor in Cleveland but was later transferred to New York. Tired of moving around, he finally accepted a post in Israel and settled there.

His wife had also been a survivor. They avoided speaking of the camps among themselves for they feared the nightmares would return. Mendel was still haunted by the same recurring dream—the children ... the forest. ...

Mendel continued his story:

I didn't go to a psychiatrist, he wouldn't have been able to help me. I receive 40 percent disability allowance for psychiatric troubles but none for physical disability, although my legs and my back still hurt as a result of the heavy labor I was forced to do in the camps.

His wife, Rivka, a small and delicate woman, was also a survivor of Auschwitz. She was at Bergen-Belsen at the time of liberation and joined her brother and sister-in-law in the United States. They, too, were camp survivors. Meeting Mendel in New York, who had lived through the same ordeals as she, gave her a sense of security. She told me the following:

An American woman, believing in the "golden way of life," would never have accepted living like we did during our first few years of marriage—we and our four little children lived in one room. Fortunately, the yeshiva supplied vegetables and other foods, for I had no money of my own. It was a hard life, but Mendel wanted to study at the yeshiva and I was not going to stop him.

Although it became easier for us later on, I continued to sew dresses for our girls and keep house.

Our seven children are now happily married. Before each of them got engaged, we visited their fiancés or fiancées parents; sometimes we liked them, sometimes we didn't, but Mendel and I generally agreed. The children were, of course, allowed to refuse our choice of partner, but they usually took our advice because they recognized that we were knowledgeable in these matters. How much does a boy whose experience is limited to studying at the yeshiva know? He trusts his parents to make the proper choice for him. Young people will mature together during the course of their married life.

I am very happy living in Israel. We used to live in a poor section of New York but had to leave after a few years. We have reached a safe harbour here. Traffic stops during Sabbath, people can walk in the streets. This isn't the case in New York, not even in Brooklyn or the Williamsburg neighborhood, where most of the residents are Jewish.

Joshua—Continuity

Joshua was sixteen years old when he arrived in Taverny. He was a gentle and mature boy with an open mind and an interest in Western culture. His tuberculosis required him to spend several months in a hospital. I had asked the Israeli Scouts to accept him in their boarding house in Southern France so that he could profit from the warm climate and use the workshops in their home.

I met him again in Israel, where he had raised a family and was the director of a home for 160 children of the Alya, which was known to be the best in the country.

His childhood in Lodz, Poland, had been a happy one. His father, a member of the congregation of the rabbi of Gour, was a businessman who was more concerned about the Talmud than about his business. The family, nevertheless, was well-off. When Germany declared war on Poland, Joshua tried to escape to the east, but it was too late. In 1940 the ghetto was already tightly secured:

I'll never forget the conduct of the Polish population. They were spiteful and hateful. They dragged Germans into our apartment and robbed and brutalized the Jews.

Soon after his arrival in the ghetto, my father fell sick and died on the day of the Jewish New Year in 1940. We were allowed to bury him in the Jewish cemetery of our town.

The head of the "Judenrat" (Jewish Council), as director of all orphanages in our community, attempted to save the Jewish children. He requisitioned the best section of the ghetto and transferred six thousand children there, including my little sister and myself. We went to school and had better food than the other inhabitants of the ghetto. To please the head of the Judenrat, who also lived in this section, we practiced military parades— one-two, one-two—during the week and marched past our "mayor" on Sundays. He was a very sick man, but he drove out to the public square in his coach and happily watched "his" children. As for us, we just loved the parades and rehearsals.

One morning, accompanied by our supervisors, we were told to assemble in the public square of the large ghetto. Many other Jews, my mother, my oldest sister, and my brothers among them, were already standing there. Large trucks were lined up, and we knew what was going to happen—an extermination camp was nearby. Although the square was tightly secured by the ghetto's Jewish policemen, the children slipped through their legs and were able to hide in the cellars. My mother, my brothers, and my older sister were deported that day and had to cross the whole town to reach the railroad junction. My older sister managed to escape during the journey and fled to Russia. Only after the war did I learn that she had found refuge in Tashkent.

Not a single child remained in the public square that evening and the Germans started their search that night. They found us all, sent us back to the orphanage, and made several head counts: there were 1,600 children. We were loaded onto carts, twenty-five or thirty at a time, guarded by Jewish policemen—one in the front and another in the back who kept telling us: *"If you run away, they will grab us instead. Please, we beg you, don't leave!"* The frightened tone of their voices was an indication that we had to fear the worst.

For two and a half days we were left in a large, empty hotel. The policemen constantly counted us, registering who left for the toilets and who came back. The supervisors bathed us, trimmed our hair, pinched our cheeks to make us look healthy, and gave us our best clothing to wear. On the way down the staircase, I tightly held my little sister's hand. An SS officer stood at the foot of the steps, and seeing our beautiful clothes and healthy looks, made us step to the right. Seventy-five of us were left standing in the courtyard, alone, unguarded. We didn't know what was going on. Then we heard trucks stopping outside and a lot of noise. Suddenly, an SS opened the door, exclaiming: *"Two are missing."* Only concerned about having the correct count, he haphazardly grabbed two children out of the group.

I was thirteen and a half years old then. They brought us back to the ghetto and confined two boys, my little sister and myself to an evacuated apartment. I don't know why, but an important looking woman in charge of distributing vegetables took a liking to me and made me run errands for her. It gave me the chance to bring home some food in the evenings. Without it, we would have starved to death.

In 1944, it was my turn to be deported and I was separated from my little sister. I knew that I would never see her again. I was sent to a work camp near Lodz. Because I was just a small boy, I was given the chore of peeling potatoes in the kitchen. Two of my father's friends were also working there and they took care of me. During our evacuation to Buchenwald, we travelled for two weeks in open railroad cars and I contracted typhus. These two men carried me from the train to the infirmary. If it hadn't been for them, I would have died.

I was still in the hospital, lying next to Naphtali, at

the time of liberation. At first, I was extremely happy to be free, but I soon realized that a curtain had been drawn over the past, and that nothing would ever bring it back. I fell into deep despair. Many of the other children experienced the same reaction and refused to continue living. In their distress, they greedily stuffed themselves with food, swallowing whole pieces of chicken; they died, deliberately.

In France, Joshua met members of the Youth Movement Yechouroun, who had established their summer camp in Ambloy. Watching these nice, young, devoted Jews who laughed and had fun together, he saw a remote chance of some day finding his own happiness himself and being able to smile again.

I don't think that I would have been able to lead a normal life right after Buchenwald. The protective atmosphere of Taverny was an indispensable stage of transition. During my psychology studies, I read Erikson and Gesell, who claim that to become an adult, a child must pass through various stages including childhood and adolescence. If he misses one, he must live through it in a different way. To me, it was restored in Taverny.

Joshua later worked as an instructor at the Scouts' home. Convinced she was doing the right thing, the head mistress concealed from him an affidavit which an aunt, a business woman in the United States, had sent. The head mistress believed that France needed instructors like Joshua. Furious about this breach of confidence, Joshua left the home to work as a counselor, first in Versailles, then in Taverny. At this time we only had children with social problems in our home. In 1952, he was sent to the Yeshiva Kol Tora in Jerusalem, and then to a training course, where he felt "the hand of God" when meeting Sara. Two years later he married her. He became chief counselor of the Jewish boarding school in Paris, studied at the university, and was nominated director of a children's home in Israel in 1956. He lives in a little house with his wife and five children.

I make every possible effort to lead a closely united, harmonious family life. It is best for my children and serves as an example to those living in the home. We follow the example of Taverny: all doors are kept open, the children may come in any time and observe us. The girls imitate whatever Sara is doing. Once married, they prepare the same cakes and cut the lemons like she does; they copy their lifestyle from ours.

Joshua mentioned the camps only to other former deported persons. Only to them, or to me, did he feel free to talk:

I went for a long time without being troubled by memories but I have started having nightmares. A psychiatrist told me that this was absolutely normal. Even after thirty-five years, a traumatic shock will bear consequences and cause nightmares. I know that this has happened to others. Many of the former deported children had forgotten this period of their life and started suffering disorders much later. I think that the Holocaust must forever remain in people's memory. What bothers me, is that during commemorative celebrations for victims of deportation, the courage of the Warsaw insurgents is highly praised. It is a great error to believe that the other deported persons only acted like sheep being led to the slaughter-house. Heroic acts were performed daily: the surveillants climbed onto the trucks without being compelled to, in order to stay with us children . . . Dr. Korcsak, the director of the Warsaw orphanage who, for the same reasons and out of his own free will, accompanied "his" 200 children to Treblinka . . . my father's friends saved my life. Heroic deeds were committed every day in the camps.

Joshua had a strong desire to pray at his father's tomb, but could not return to Poland because of his Israeli passport. Yet, he has not lost all hope. He had experienced the death of his family differently from others—the tomb of his father exists,he said goodbye to his mother—and therefore, could indulge in his grief consciously, without bearing the terrible sense of guilt of having survived.

Joshua chose to be an instructor, thus continuing the same lifestyle he had known as a child and adolescent—a community life rather than a family life. The protective atmosphere of collective living was familiar to him. He saw nothing unusual in the delayed effects of deportation, as they were shared by many Israeli citizens who resembled him.

Chapter Eleven

Famous People

Elie Wiesel, Writer—Memories

Elie, now a noted writer, and Daniel, now a famous scientist, were close friends in Ambloy. Together, they were instructed by private teachers who prepared them for school. The teachers were fascinated by the insatiable intellectual curiosity of the two young men who, within one year, learned French and were ready to enter high school.

After finishing his studies, Elie became the Paris correspondent for the Israeli newspaper *Yedioth A'haronot*. In his small, rented room he worked for the newspaper and continued to study the Talmud.

Elie Wiesel's career as a writer is worth mentioning. During the fifties, the President of France, Pierre Mendès-France had successfully ended the Indochina War and was at the height of his popularity. The head of the Israeli daily newspaper wanted to print an interview with him, but President Mendès-France had never granted an interview during his time in office. Elie tried his luck with Francois Mauriac, a fervent defender of the French president during his battles with envious criticizers and, often enough, his political enemies. Mauriac agreed to see the young reporter.

Francois Mauriac's intellectual curiosity, combined with the sympathy he felt for Wiesel, added a personal dimension to their conversation. The tragic events in the young man's life were bound to touch such a sensitive man as Francois

Mauriac. He, however, associated those events with cliches of the Catholic spiritual world: suffering, grace and redemption. Shocked by this attitude, Elie was about to end the interview and leave, but Francois Mauriac begged him to stay. Elie explained to him that he could not accept the belittlement of his and many others' ordeals or their reduction to a divine mystery with moral tendencies. Francois Mauriac listened to him, asked him questions, and encouraged Wiesel to relay his experiences to the public at large. In short, he prompted him to write a book (with a preface by Mauriac) which was published by the "Editions de Minuit" in 1958. Their friendship became a lasting and solid one. Many years later, when Wiesel's works were awarded the "Prix Médicis," honoring the best foreign author whose works were in French, the illustrious old man came to the Editions du Seuil to congratulate Elie Wiesel, whom he considered a younger brother.

Elie waited until the end of the fifties to cross the Atlantic ocean. He had no intention of settling in America but was forced to extend his stay in a hospital there because of an automobile accident. His French visa expired while he was recuperating and he ended up staying in the United States where he enjoys an ever-increasing audience.

As a writer, journalist, lecturer, and professor, Wiesel's works encompass the complexity of Jewish destiny, revolving around the Hassidic background of his forefathers. Yet, he does not stay within the restrictive walls of pedantic dogma. He is deeply concerned about the fate of his people, everywhere in the world, be it in Israel, the United States, the USSR, or the United Nations. His book, *Jews of Silence,* has been very influential. Its worldwide impact has made a breach in the iron curtain, thus enabling 150,000 Jews to emigrate to the free world. His travels take him around the globe, his address—as Isaac Navon, former president of the Jewish State declared when handing him a prize—is the universe. He is the omni-present, talented defender of his brothers.

Elie Wiesel is concerned about the fate of all oppressed people in the world. Unlike some members of the Jewish movement, who are often interested soley in the fate of the Jewish people, Wiesel gets personally involved in defending blacks and fighting oppression in Latin America. He was also a participant in the march against hunger in Cambodia.

His relationship with high-ranking officials of the United States administration, especially with former President Carter, permits him to plead more effectively and to have a stronger influence on his audiences. He does not restrict himself to the role of a talented memorialist, though he accepted to head the U.S. Holocaust Memorial Council in Washington, D.C., a group formed to prevent the Jewish catastrophe from being associated with other oppressions, as monstrous as they may be.

To him, the persecution of the Jews not only represents the final rejection of his brothers, his species, but also implies the annihilation of his fellow-man. Here is what he told me:

> *Deportation must never be forgotten. I have taken it upon myself to keep it in everyone's memory. Yet, although I mention the camps during my conferences, I cannot describe what happened there. For many years, I was unable to pronounce the word "Auschwitz." I teach human relations at Boston University where more students sign up for my lectures than I can accept. But I'll never refuse admittance to the children of my former friends of Taverny, who, in their distress and incapacity to speak about their pasts, send them to me. They want me to explain the Hassidic movement to them, the actions of the Holy Sect that disappeared in the fire, as it could not subsist in our undeserving world.*
>
> *I watched the movie* Holocaust *on television. It was an insult to those who had been deported. It distorted the facts of life in concentration camps. What disturbs me even more is that I was the one to introduce the term "holocaust" in one of my books. Actually, I don't even like the word, but now everyone has adopted it. "Holocaust" is, in fact, the word for a consentual sacrifice, whereas the one we are speaking about was a catastrophe ("Shoah" in Hebrew). The correct term is "genocide."*

135

The word "readjustment" does not apply to this sensitive man who has voiced so strongly the distress he and so many others have suffered. I believe, however, that the birth of his son Elisha, who bears his father's name, has marked an important point in Elie's life. He explained the reason he married so late in life:

> *I hesitated for a long time to have a child because of my pessimistic views of the world. Today, my child is my most precious possession. Raising him reminds me of the relationship that I had with my father. My father, however, spoke very little, leaving me to guess his feelings and intentions. I, on the other hand, discuss many topics with Elisha, and take him along on my journeys. He is enrolled in a Jewish school where he receives a traditional education.*

By raising a family, Elie demonstrated that his trust in the future overruled the hopelessness caused by his past experiences. Like most of his comrades of Taverny, he faced the challenge—and won.

Daniel—Positivism

Elie Wiesel's friend, Daniel, is professor of physics at New York University and strictly observes the Jewish religion. He is a modest, yet famous scientist whose advice is largely sought. His father had been deported and died of exhaustion. His oldest brother disappeared; his mother died in Auschwitz.

> *In 1943, at the age of 14, I came to the camp with my little 12-year-old brother, Meyer. We stayed together until liberation. I wouldn't be alive if it had not been for Meyer for he always managed to find some food. He kept me from losing all hope, and, in a way, forced me to survive.*
>
> *I had always liked mathematics and started studying as soon as I arrived in France. One year later, Elie and I tried to pass our baccalaureate certificates, but I failed*

136

because of my inadequate knowledge of French.

We found members of our families in the United States and, although we were reluctant, embarked on the Exodus. We felt very lonely in New York. Undertaking regular studies was impossible because we didn't speak a word of English.

Daniel entered a yeshiva and picked up a few words of English here and there. He entered a university in 1949 and worked at odd jobs to pay his way. He was a bell-boy, delivery-boy and errand-boy in a drugstore. He obtained a degree in physics in 1952 but, lacking U.S. citizenship, was unable to find a job. He continued working at the drugstore for a few dollars a week.

In 1953, five years after his arrival in the United States, Daniel became an American citizen—an event that changed his life. He obtained a job in the Navy laboratories and kept it for twelve years,while persuing his studies at the university.

I am very grateful to this country for the trust it has put in me. As soon as I became an American citizen, I was granted atomic clearance and was allowed to do extensive research work in Washington where I learned about existing weapons. The unrestrictive trust the U.S. puts in their citizens is very unusual.

I soon started earning three thousand dollars a year, but I wasn't really interested in money, no more than I was in diplomas, degrees or doctorates. I never took part in any graduation ceremonies. I believe that this is an aftereffect of my life in the camps. Without it, I would never have undertaken anything other than religious studies for they were the only ones our family accepted. In a way, the deportation was a very positive experience for me, for it happened while I was still very young. I believe that the camps have had a strong influence on my present life, although I hardly think of them now. One dream keeps coming back, though. It concerns the last day before liberation when I had gone into hiding while others were being shot outside of the barracks.

Nothing is as terrible as the fear of the unknown.

In 1955 I married the daughter of a rabbi. From that day on, my social life changed. People look at married men differently. My wife and I have three sons. I don't get involved in their education, which makes my wife very unhappy. I neither help them with their advanced Jewish studies nor with their regular schooling. I feel that they must manage by themselves and are free to decide whether they want to continue studying, or whether they want to do nothing at all. I have the same attitude with my students. At the beginning of my lectures, I try to impress them with my knowledge, but I don't interfere after that.

Because of my accent, of course, my students know that I am not from this country. I told them that I came from Poland. During the summer, when it is too warm to wear a coat, they see my tattooed number. I don't hide anything from them, but I never speak openly about the past. I don't discuss it with my children either, in spite of their many questions. I am totally absorbed in my scientific research work and have a very interesting life.

I have often blamed myself for intruding into the intimacy of the survivors' private lives and stirring up painful memories. Daniel, however, reassured me that I had not—speaking had relieved him:

I usually do not open up but it made me very happy that you gave me the opportunity to speak so freely about myself.

Chapter Twelve

Determined to Live

The stories relayed in this book clearly show that concentration camp life had its impact on each of the survivors, changing each of them in some way. Some of them were weakened while others grew stronger.

Each of the statements is a personal, yet different story, for each of the survivors experienced a different childhood, a different camp life. It would be absurd to generalize, yet, it seems that those who were deported when they were very young demonstrated a common strength. What impressed me most of all was their determination to survive and to perpetuate life.

After they were freed from the camps, there were two possible options for the survivors. The first option was to continue living "as before": the survivor would choose his father's trade, marry a girl of his own social standing (whether she had been deported or not), and give his children the same education that he had received. The second possibility was for the survivor to plan only for the future, marry a girl who had never heard about the camps, and raise his children without referring to his own childhood.

Surprisingly enough, no matter what option they chose, all of the survivors have kept silent about their pasts, never evoking them. "We don't like to scrape at the protective crust," one of them said.

We will find no definite common denominator by studying the survivors' stories according to the country they chose to settle in. Yet, it seems that in France, where only a few survivors from Taverny live, they have attempted to blend into the masses. In the United States, however, they have often decided to either become full-fledged citizens by marrying an American woman of longtime stock and possibly deleting the tattooed numbers from their arms, or to segregate into special sections in an attempt to recreate the image of communities destroyed in Europe.

In the Holy Land, where the survivors represent a large group within the entire population, they seem to have had less difficulty overcoming their pasts. They have been able to express their aggression in a constructive way—by contributing to the birth of the State of Israel.

As a whole, to young people who were able to translate their emotions into actions—determination to avenge, to fight, to testify—survival had greater meaning than to those who felt that they had survived only "by accident" or "by chance."

Another important factor in the process of reintegration was the age at which the youngsters were deported. We have noticed that of the two brothers who were deported together, the younger brother adapted more easily to camp life and encountered fewer problems than the older one. A close examination of the statements definitely discloses that the decisive factor was the age at which the youngest had been deported.

In my opinion, the young survivors can be separated into four age groups:

a) The very young children who were deported and liberated before the age of eight or nine, did not remember the period before the camps and believed that their childhood had been normal. Although their reintegration was often painful, as they generally were without any family, they succeeded in reaching a social standing.

b) Children who were deported later in life, liberated between 12 and 14 years of age, remembered their childhood and definitely suffered a lasting traumatic shock. They were not yet discriminating enough to judge their jailors or even their fellow inmates. They generally adapted well to life in the camps and frequently were the ones to help their older brothers. At the end of the war, though, things changed for them. Not having fully developed their personalities yet, integration into society often was very problematic. They had to bear the stigma of concentration camp life throughout their life. Married or not, they remained outsiders.

c) Then there were the adolescents, aged 15 to 19, who reached an age of understanding in the camps. After liberation, they were able to shake off negative impressions. If they had a flexible, yet strong personality, they were able to "start anew" and, in many cases,the sufferings they had endured strengthened them.

d) The survivors of 20 to 24 years of age had similar attitudes to adults. Planning for the future was very hard for them because out of nostalgia they wanted to adhere to traditional values, without endangering their reintegration into society.

The Second Generation

Most of the survivors grew up with a harmonious family life. But what about their children?

I was amazed to notice a similar attitude in all children of victims of deportation, whether their parents had disappeared in the death camps or had survived concentration camp ordeals. They shared the unknown, the unspoken, the severance of a thread that had united many generations. The former boys of Taverny kept sending their offspring to me from all over the world so that I could reveal the story of their parents or their grandparents, who were unable to speak about it themselves. These children admired their parents for the courage they showed during and after camp life. But they, themselves, cannot endure the consequences of a collective tragedy.

Once they have become adolescents, these young people never fail to recognize each other on a campus, in the Army, or during gatherings. Their behavior makes it evident: they keep to themselves, observe the others, speak very little and never mention their families, despite the excellent education most of them have received. They instinctively group together, since among themselves their differences are not as obvious as when they are with others. This is why they have founded various associations in Israel, the United States, and France: "The Sons and Daughters of Victims of Deportation." They form the majority of the audience at international conferences about "deportation and its consequences" or at Elie Wiesel's lectures.

The parents' foremost desire is to have happy, healthy children without any special problems, children who are not different from the others.

Without generalizing, I want to try to explain this phenomenon by relaying my neighbor's story. She came to me spontaneously when she heard that I was writing this book:

Nothing has been written about the frequent disorders of children of victims of deportation, who, even as adults, often present serious psychological disturbances. The disorders stem from two periods in the child's life: before his parents' deportation and after. Whatever the age of the child, the period "before" forever remains in his memory or imagination as a time of "paradise lost." Whether or not one or both parents disappeared, the period "after" they return is bound to bring forth painful symptoms.

I would like to talk about a case where the mother disappeared and the father, after surviving Auschwitz, raised his two children by himself. An atmosphere of distress surrounded the home which could not be dispelled by the apparent richness of the household. Photos of deportations were left within reach of the children; their young minds were encumbered with commemorative literature lining the book shelves.

The father felt guilty for the mother's absence. He was a hard worker who, in spite of his melancholic crises, attempted to overcome his distress by a positive attitude and by trying to be successful in his work. Children of survivors, out of a sense of compensation, are generally spoiled by their parents. But even the affection surrounding these particular children could not make them forget that they were orphans, and, most of all, that they were unprepared to master their lives. The children constantly evoked the death camps, picturing themselves living in Auschwitz. They were restless, showing an almost morbidly exaggerated sensitivity. They saw enemies, traitors, possible anti-Semites everywhere and were constantly on the alert.

At age 12, the little girl would not go to bed without hiding a revolver under her pillow. Still, her sleep was haunted by fearful nightmares. She sought refuge in a dreamworld that she had to abandon as soon as she encountered the realities of life, her whole fictitious world crumbling to pieces.

Due to the absence of the mother and the father's weird behavior, the brother and sister were very close to each other. The brother, being the older of the two, believed that he would be the "head of the family" soon, as the father did nothing to dispel the hovering threat of his imminent death, thus nourishing the children's sense of insecurity. They were always surrounded by adults; when expressing the wish to meet children of their own age, they were told: "They are all dead." Because they worshipped the memory of their dead mother and assisted at innumerable commemorative ceremonies, they were convinced that they were different from others.

A secret hostility against their father grew in the depth of the children's unconscious minds. They found him "guilty" of surrounding them with dark

143

memories, but at the same time idolized him as a hero who was weakened by his sufferings endured in the camps. They lived in the constant fear of losing him, of becoming full orphans.

Thus, at a very tender age, the little girl showed a deep fear of death, of the cold, and of other people's hostilities. She took refuge in a fictitious religious world, seeing God as the supreme redeemer. Later on, she escaped her memories and obsessions by falling ill.

Because of her father's irate and suspicious temper, she became an awkward, unsociable person. She felt guilty to be alive while her mother was dead. Also, because she resembled her mother, she saw a constant reproach in her father's unsteady yet angry eyes. She was totally indifferent to her surroundings, yet, by nature, she was a very affectionate girl. In addition to this dilemma, she blamed herself for being sick, and a terrible void and sense of isolation invaded her whole being, affecting even her conscious mind.

At the time her parents were deported, the little girl was eleven months old, the boy nine years. Later, he told his sister that in his nightmares he imagined himself to be strong enough to defend his parents. He had been away from home when his parents were arrested; the little girl was saved in time by neighbors. A Christian woman was put in charge of her and took care of her as best she could. The little girl grew very fond of her and when the father returned after two and a half years, the foster-mother even offered him money in exchange for the little girl. The boy, at that time, was with a group of Jewish children who had been hidden by peasants.

The children were terribly shocked to see their ghastly-looking, unrecognizable father, weighing only 80 pounds. To the little girl whom he frantically hugged and kissed, he was nothing but a frightful stranger. The boy was sad to see his beloved father

144

in such a condition and it deeply afflicted him that he had lost his mother.

The family had to be rebuilt from scratch and the father constantly spoke of his imminent death, impressing upon the boy that he would have to care for his little sister. She was sent to several boarding houses, but she never stayed very long. Scared to be left home alone, she would run over to the neighbors' house or, tightly wrapped in a blanket, would be taken to the room of one of the servants.

She was then adopted by a family that had known her mother, and spent a few happy years with them. But her family instinct overruled and she returned to her father and brother, convinced that it was her duty to stay with them, that they needed her. Her years as an adolescent were very much disturbed; no truly feminine counseling had prepared her for life. The boy was more or less successful in school. As for the girl, she buried herself in books, in a world of fiction which suited her poetic nature. An infinite need for love made her wait for "Prince Charming," and she invested every inch of her romantic nature when she fell in love for the first time. Thus, when she was deceived, she broke down. She sought the aid of psychiatrists and psychotherapists. By the time she was twenty she was a drug addict, swallowing anti-depressive and tranquilizing pills and submitting herself to electro-shock treatments. After many more delusions, she ended up marrying at the age of 36 and seemed to have found peace of mind. Yet, soon after, she had to be admitted to a hospital.

Recurring visions of terror haunted her. She imagined herself in a concentration camp where she would be killed. Her world consisted of hostility and danger and people who were bad and full of underlying aggression. The terrible blanket of silence that was spread over Auschwitz seemed to confirm her convictions. She had a completely dis-

145

turbed attitude towards food, swallowing enormous quantities without feeling satiated. Searching for the hero who would resemble her father, she married relatively late, trying to find in her husband a substitute for her mother. They had children, but her role of mother was an ever-growing burden to her as she was unable to identify herself with her own mother whom she had never known.

Her brother, at the age of fifty, had not married, searching in vain for a non-existent woman: his mother. He surrounded himself with a group of faithful friends, who protected him like a bodyguard, and never went anywhere without his shepherd dog and collected hunting guns.

While she was young, the girl ardently wished to be a boy so that she would have the strength to defend herself in case of war. Yet, she yearned for affection and kindness, abhorring violence to the point of having nightmares. She was an avid reader of books and documents concerning the fate of the Jewish people, searching to understand her father with a morbid curiosity; she felt deeply sorry for him. The three of them—father, daughter, and son—were united by a tight bond of tragedy. The pain of one was felt by the others.

Observing the "second generation," we realize that the characteristic attitude of survivors—anxiety, fear of separation, incapacity to enjoy life, a sense of guilt—has often played a destructive role in their children's lives who, in spite of respecting their parents, feel sorry for them. They refrain from leading independent lives for fear of hurting their parents' feelings. They completely lack a sense of security and thus cannot develop their own personality. They have inherited their parents' distress.

This anguish subsists throughout the years and is even found in the "third generation." The children of survivors, consciously or unconsciously, use the same attitude towards their own children that their parents had used towards them. Delayed effects . . . Echoes of deportation . . .

CONCLUSION

While I was in the United States I visited my uncle, the noted rabbi Joseph Breuer, who is 97 years old and blind. I explained to him why I had come to New York and told him about the testimonies of the boys of Taverny. I asked him straight out: "Many people believe that enough has been said about the deportations, that history has known many exterminations of the Jewish people: after the ruin of the second temple, during the Crusades, Chmielnitzki in 1648, Kitchiney at the end of the last century.... There have been no more deportations for 38 years; has the time come to stop talking about them?"

After a long moment of silence, my uncle replied: "You may be right, someday we will have to cease talking about them. But I do not know when. I believe that as long as a single deported person, a single camp survivor is still alive, we must continue to speak up, so that he may feel less isolated and better understood."

Yes, many of them are still alive, although their number diminishes daily.

The Germans had drawn up detailed lists with the names of 6,361,000 deported Jews; the exact number of survivors, however, is not known, nor are their names. We know how miserable and exhausted these poor people were at the time of liberation, but we were told no more.

Freud wrote in 1919 that a traumatic experience always leaves traces which diminish over the years. The effects of war-neuroses generally disappear after one or two years.[1]

[1]Freud, S. Introduction to Psycho-Analysis and War-Neuroses. Standard Edition, 17, London, Hogarth Press, 1955.

147

This however, does not apply to the traumatic effects of deportation. Camp survivors, just as survivors of Hiroshima, are marked forever by their experiences.[1]

Everyone expected that, after regaining their strength, the survivors would seek vengeance on the German population. It would have seemed normal that they kill, pillage, rebel, and cry for justice.

Nothing of the sort happened, though. Not only did they refrain from taking any action, they remained unusually passive, and they kept silent. . . . Yet, many of the survivors declared that they had resolved to survive in order to serve as eye-witnesses of what had happened, and to prevent the death and the sufferings of their families from being forever lost in historic oblivion.[2]

After liberation, they did not cry out, they did not speak. The silence that veiled the existence of the camps from the beginning has persisted long after.[3]

Silence after such tragedy is a common phenomenon. It is easy to understand why the Germans have kept the secret: they preferred to pretend that the camps did not exist.[4] But how about the victims? How can their silence be explained? Indeed, only a few of them were able to describe the horrible, frightful scenes they had witnessed. And the few who have tried to speak were not believed; they soon realized that it was impossible to impart the meaning of deportation and concentration camp life. Most of all, however, their physical and psychological injuries, the humiliation of having been no more than a number, and the guilt of having survived while all members of their families died were such that they were unable to express their inner feelings—and this has not changed to this date.

This is the reason that in Taverny, neither Niny or myself could fully comprehend the extent of the psychological trauma, of the sufferings endured by the young people, and

[1]Lifton, N.J. The Survivors of the Hiroshima disaster and the Survivors of Nazi Persecution, in Massive Psychic Trauma, Krystal, H. ed., New York, Int. Univ. Press, 1968.
[2]Pisar, S. Ke sang de l'espoir, paris, Laffon, 1979.
[3]Wiesel, E. Entre deux soleils, Paris, Seuil, 1970.
[4]Kagon, E. L'Etat SS, Paris, Laffon, 1979.

148

were unaware of the uniqueness of their "surviving." We were far from realizing that we were witnessing a historic era. Being of about the same age, we understood that we had narrowly escaped deportation and death ourselves, and we felt very humble. We accepted the boys as they were, simply trusting them without trying to force anything upon them.

I decided to write this book because I am proud of them and of what they have achieved; I admire their courage and their strength. Their story had to be revealed to the world. But should I have been the one to relate it? Should I have left this task to them?

The effects of deportation have left indelible marks on the survivors; their only chance to live is by keeping silent, by burying the past deep within themselves. That is why I have taken it upon myself to speak in their behalf. I have recorded their testimonies, yet, I fear that I may have distorted certain facts, that I may have misinterpreted some of their feelings. I therefore ask those who are mentioned in this book to forgive me if, unintentionally, I misunderstood their reactions or the manner in which they see themselves.

Each of the testimonies relays the story of an often rich life, which concerns and affects us all. Perhaps these testimonies can give voice to others who are yet unable to speak about the past. And we must feel deep sorrow for all the children and young people who have died in the camps and who will forever remain silent.